TRUE CHAMPIONS KNOW WHAT IT TAKES
TO LIVE A VICTORIOUS LIFE

INTEGRITY

CHAD BONHAM, GENERAL EDITOR

FELLOWSHIP OF
CHRISTIAN ATHLETES

THE HEART AND SOUL IN SPORTS

Regal

From Gospel Light
Ventura, California, U.S.A.

Published by Regal
From Gospel Light
Ventura, California, U.S.A.
www.regalbooks.com
Printed in the U.S.A.

Library of Congress Cataloging-in-Publication Data
Integrity / Fellowship of Christian Athletes.
p. cm.
ISBN-13: 978-0-8307-4580-7 (trade paper)
1. Athletes—Religious life. 2. Integrity—Religious aspects—Christianity.
I. Fellowship of Christian Athletes.
BV4596.A8I58 2008
241'.4—dc22
2008011572

1 2 3 4 5 6 7 8 9 10 / 15 14 13 12 11 10 09 08

Rights for publishing this book outside the U.S.A. or in non-English
languages are administered by Gospel Light Worldwide, an international
not-for-profit ministry. For additional information, please visit www.glww.org,
email info@glww.org, or write to Gospel Light Worldwide,
1957 Eastman Avenue, Ventura, CA 93003, U.S.A.

CONTENTS

THE FOUR CORE

Dan Britton
Senior Vice President of Ministries, Fellowship of Christian Athletes

The NCAA Final Four tournament is an exciting sporting event. Even if you are not a person who likes basketball, it is awesome to watch March Madness as it narrows down 64 teams into 4 core teams. This makes me think about Fellowship of Christian Athlete's "Four Core"—not four core teams, but four core values.

Core values are simply the way you live and conduct yourself. They are your attitudes, beliefs and convictions. Values should be what you are, not what you want to become. The goal is to embody your values every step of the way.

Are your values just words, or do you actually live them out? Can others identify the values in your life without your telling them? Your values need to be a driving force that shapes the way you do life! Talk is cheap, but values are valuable.

When everything is stripped away, what is left? For FCA, it is integrity, serving, teamwork and excellence. These Four Core are so powerful to me that I have made them my own personal values. So, I have to ask you, what are your values? What guides you? Let me share with you FCA's Four Core, which are even better than the Final Four!

Integrity

To have integrity means that you are committed to Christ-like wholeness, both privately and publicly. Basically, it means to live without gaps. Proverbs 11:3 says that integrity should guide you, but that a double life will destroy you. You need to be transparent, authentic, honest and trustworthy. You should be the same in all situations and not become someone different when the competition of the game begins. Integrity means to act the same when no one is looking. It is not about being perfect, but, as a coach or athlete, you need to be the real deal.

Serving

In John 13:12-15, Jesus gives us the perfect example of serving when He washes the disciples' feet. He then commands the disciples to go and do unto others what He has done to them. How many of your teammates' feet have you washed? Maybe not literally, but spiritually, do you have an attitude of serving just as if you were washing their feet in the locker room? You need to seek out the needs of others and be passionate about pursuing people who are needy. And, the last time I checked, everyone is needy.

Teamwork

Teamwork means to work together with others and express unity in Christ in all of your relationships. In Philippians 2:1-5, Paul encourages each of us to be one, united together in spirit and purpose. We all need to be on one team—not just the team we play on, but on God's Team! We need to equip, encourage and empower one another. Do you celebrate and hurt together as teammates? You need to be arm-in-arm with others, locking up together to accomplish God's work. There should be no Lone Rangers.

Excellence

To pursue excellence means to honor and glorify God in everything you do. In Colossians 3:23-24, Paul writes, "whatever you do, work at it with all your heart, as working for the Lord, not for men." The "whatever" part is hard, because it means that everything you do must be done for God, not others. You need to pursue excellence in practice, in games, in schoolwork and in lifting weights. God deserves your best, not your leftovers.

It is tip-off time for the game of life. How will you be known?

Whatever happens, conduct yourselves in a manner worthy of the gospel of Christ.
PHILIPPIANS 1:27, *NIV*

Lord Jesus, my prayer is to live and compete with integrity, serving, teamwork and excellence. It is a high standard, but I know that with Your power and strength, it can happen. I want all my relationships to be known for things that are of You. Search my heart and reveal to me my values. I lay at the foot of the cross the values that do not honor You, and I ask for Your forgiveness. The values that bring You glory, I lay them at the foot of the cross for Your anointing.

THE GAP

I know, my God, that you test the heart and are pleased with integrity.
All these things have I given willingly and with honest intent.

1 CHRONICLES 29:17

The core value of integrity is more than the classic defini-tion of "who we are when no one is watching." Integrity is a value that we need to pursue, even when it is not conven-ient. It ultimately defines us. Our talk, decisions, thoughts and actions are built on our integrity.

Integrity takes a lifetime to build and a second to lose. We are always one decision away from being stupid. When we maintain a life of integrity, there is wholeness of soul. There is spiritual and emotional rest.

There are no spiritual shortcuts to integrity. Being com-mitted to live out daily what we believe takes spiritual sweat. As legendary Hall of Fame basketball coach John Wooden once said, "A leader's most powerful ally is his or her own example. There is hypocrisy to the phrase, 'Do as I say, not as I do.' I refused to make demands on my boys that I wasn't willing to live out in my own life."

Integrity is not about being perfect, but about being transparent and authentic. Sometimes non-believers have more integrity than Christians. For them, it is "what you see is what you get!" They do not hide anything. The world is dying to see authentic followers of Christ. God desires for us to have spiritual authenticity, not spiritual duplicity.

Too often, we desire to live a life that we know we have not committed in our hearts to living. We also want others to do as we say, not as we do. What I mean by this is that we desire for our external life (the life that everyone sees—our wins and accomplishments) to be greater than our internal life (the life that no one sees—our thoughts and desires).

The two key ingredients of integrity are honesty and truth. When these become merely an option and not a non-negotiable standard, gaps develop in our integrity, and hypocrisy is born. The best definition of "hypocrisy" I have ever heard is that it is "the gap that exists between the public life and the private life." It is the difference between the external life and the internal life.

There is a constant war in our souls. We do not want others to see us as we really are. We are afraid that the gap will be exposed. However, God desires the exact opposite. He wants us to bring the dark things—the things that we have buried in our hearts—into the light so that He can purify us. He wants every aspect of our lives to be filled with integrity.

Oswald Chambers once wrote, "My worth to God in public is only what I am in private." Be committed to being real—gap free!

How to Use this Book

Integrity takes an in-depth look at this core value and comes at it from 12 different angles as lived out by 12 different people. Their insights shed new light on this value and give us a model to follow.

You can read *Integrity* individually or as part of a group. As part of a personal devotion time, you can gain insight as you read through each story and ponder on the "Training Time" questions at the end. Mentors can also use this book in a discipleship relationship, using the "Training Time" questions to step up to the next level. And small groups (huddles) can study the core value as a group to be prepared to sharpen each other with questions.

1

The Quest for Consistency

Tony Dungy

Winning Super Bowl Coach of the Indianapolis Colts

Remember your leaders who have spoken God's word to you.
As you carefully observe the outcome of their lives, imitate their faith.
Jesus Christ is the same yesterday, today, and forever.

HEBREWS 13:7-8

It is not what we eat but what we digest that makes us strong;
not what we gain but what we save that makes us rich; not what we
read but what we remember that makes us learned; and not what
we profess but what we practice that gives us integrity.

FRANCIS BACON

Living in full view of the microscopic public eye can test the will of even the strongest of characters. Tony Dungy can certainly attest to that brutal truth. As the celebrated head coach of the Indianapolis Colts, he's experienced the pinnacle of success, the most tragic of personal losses and everything in between.

For the average Joe, experiencing a few highs and lows with nondescript days in between is simply called "life."

But for Dungy—when every detail is reported, discussed, prognosticated and opined—life is something completely different and looks more like a virtual three-ring circus in which triumphs and defeats are fodder for the masses.

That's why integrity is so vital in the life of the Christian. After all, everyone is in the public eye to some degree, with followers of Christ attracting much of the scrutinizing spotlight. And that's what makes Dungy so special. His integrity is unwavering, his character rock solid—no matter what circumstance comes his way. It's a quality that people can't help but notice from up close and from far away.

"The greatest things I have learned from Coach Dungy would have to be humility and consistency," Indianapolis tight end Ben Utecht says. "He truly leads by example, and he does it consistently. This allows people to really see his faith every single day, and that's the most important thing."

Not only do his players recognize Dungy's steady approach, but the men and women who cover the national sports scene also are amazed at his impeccable commitment to doing the right thing.

"Tony Dungy is probably the most even-keeled person I have ever met," ESPN anchor Chris Berman says. "In the span of just over a year, he experienced a personal low that can get no lower—the tragic death of his son—and the professional high that can be no higher—winning the Super Bowl. The way he carried himself in both situations, you wouldn't know the difference, really, in what event just occurred. I don't know many people who could do that. I love him for his fortitude and his unbelievable ability to stay the course."

"Tony is a man of such inner strength that you can't help but be inspired by him," ESPN *Monday Night Football* reporter Michelle Tafoya adds. "He is consistent, composed and compassionate. I've never met another coach like him, and I don't expect to. From Tony, I have learned that you can be successful while maintaining your integrity, that you can be composed while being competitive, and that you can leave a legacy based on character."

Those strong words are echoed by countless others and reflect the sentiment of people who have observed Dungy's nearly 30 years within the coaching ranks. Amazingly, all but one year of his entire career have taken place inside the demanding confines of the National Football League, where coaches are required to spend 80 hours a week on the job just to have a sniff at success and where character and integrity are challenged on a daily basis.

Yet somehow, Dungy has served as a head coach since 1996 and managed not only to maintain a high standard of integrity but also to become a role model of character for coaches and athletes at every level of competition—from the Pee Wee League all the way to the NFL.

"Integrity, to me, is what you are all about," Dungy says. "It's what's inside of you. And what's inside is eventually going to come out when it gets to a critical situation. That, to me, is the difference between a championship team and just a good team. That's the difference between a person you really want to follow and someone who is just another person in your life. With people of integrity, you know what you are going to get because that person is the same way all the time; situations don't change them. That's what I look for in players, and that's what I want to give players from a leadership standpoint—that they can count on me to be the same no matter what. Being the same is not just being mediocre. It's really being the person that God wants you to be all the time."

Dungy's legacy of integrity began not as a coach but as a player. The Michigan native was the starting quarterback at the University of Minnesota from 1973 to 1976 and spent his freshman season playing on the basketball team as well. As a free agent, he signed with the Pittsburgh Steelers as a defensive back. He was later converted to wide receiver and then to safety. In his second season, Dungy took part in the Steelers' 35-31 victory over Dallas in Super Bowl XIII.

After two years in Pittsburgh and one year in San Francisco, Dungy returned to his alma mater to coach the defensive backs for a season. By 1981, he was back in the NFL for good. After assistant coaching stints in Pittsburgh, Kansas City and Minnesota, his sphere of influence expanded when he was named head coach of the Tampa Bay Buccaneers. And while the demands on his life increased, so too did notice of his ability to display grace under fire. The assistant coaches and support staff that surrounded him were particularly quick to see this.

One of those impressionable coworkers was Les Steckel, who served as Tony Dungy's offensive coordinator in Tampa Bay for the 2000 season. Steckel, who is now president of the Fellowship of Christian Athletes, learned quickly how his former boss's word consistently reflected his integrity—so much so that he never questioned anything Dungy said.

"Someone had told me that Tony had memorized the book of James," Steckel recalls. "I went up to Tony after practice one day during the summer and I said, 'Hey, Tony, I hear you memorized the book of James this summer.' And he said, 'Yeah.' That's all he said, and I didn't ask him anything else. He said, 'Yeah,' and I believed him."

After turning the Buccaneers organization into a winner (even falling just six points shy of a berth in Super Bowl XXXIV), he was sought out by Indianapolis Colts' owner Jim Irsay to replace Jim Mora. Irsay says that Dungy reminded him of the legendary Dallas Cowboys' coach Tom Landry. He was impressed by Dungy's ability to win with integrity and saw him as the visionary who could lead the Colts to the NFL's Promised Land.

"The most important quality for any head coach is to be the leader of men," Irsay says. "Tony has those qualities. He never shies away from difficult circumstances. He's very pragmatic in terms of the way he looks at things. He has a lot of street smarts, and he's extremely competitive. The fires burn in there deeply, and people demonstrate that in different ways. But he's as competitive as

Lombardi or any coach who might have been more outward with their emotions. He's very intelligent. He has a great understanding of the game. He grew up under great teachers, so all of those things were there to give him the pedigree to make him a Hall of Fame NFL coach."

While Dungy would surely blush at Irsay's words of praise, he would also be hard pressed to reject his team-owner's assertion that integrity and consistency play a vital role in the success of any coach. Dungy says that holds especially true with more experienced athletes who require larger doses of trust in their leaders.

"Sometimes I think when you're dealing with younger players—junior high, high school—they're going to follow the coach because he's the authority figure," Dungy says. "They've been taught that they just have to follow that adult figure. But when you're dealing with professional athletes and college athletes, that goes out the window. They're going to follow you because they believe in you, and they see something that causes them to follow you. So I think it's even more important for us to build those relationships for our players and to not be anything different than they think we are because they're not going to buy into it, and they're not going to follow you wholeheartedly if there are any chinks in the armor."

For Dungy, his intense desire to live a life of integrity began at an early age. His parents, Dr. Wilbur and CleoMae Dungy, were both educators in Jackson, Michigan, where Dungy was born and raised. Although both have since passed on, their example of honesty, character and integrity continues to inspire him to always do what's right in the eyes of God.

While coaching in Tampa, Dungy took his commitment to integrity within the family a step further by helping cofound a program called All Pro Dads—a division of a larger organization known as Family First. The group hosts special events at various NFL stadiums and encourages fathers to step up their commitment in the home. Taking part in such an organization is a natural extension of the kind of parent Dungy strives to be in his own family.

"It's very important to let my family know that here are our standards," Dungy says. "Here are the Lord's standards. This is what we're going to try to live up to. Sure we're going to fail at times. We're going to fall short. But this is our role model. This is what we're all about. This is what people can expect to see hopefully all the time. And I think that's very important. Your family sees a lot more of you than your players do. If you're not totally transparent, and if you're not totally honest and have that integrity at home, then it's going to show up sooner there than it does at work."

During the 2005 season, Dungy's integrity as a father was put to an unexpected and life-altering test. His oldest son, James, who was attending college in Tampa at the time, took his own life. The quest for a Super Bowl title suddenly came to a screeching halt as Dungy was forced to temporarily step away from his duties as head coach and focus all of his energy on being the spiritual leader of his heartbroken home.

At James's funeral, Dungy showed incredible poise and grace. Hundreds of family members, friends and associates (past and present) marveled at the peace that enveloped this grieving father. After the service, Les Steckel recalls a brief encounter with Dungy. The two embraced, and Dungy whispered into his friend's ear, "Nobody told me being a Christian would be this hard."

In his book *Quiet Strength: The Principles, Practices, and Priorities of a Winning Life,* Dungy admits later feeling as if his credibility as spokesman for All Pro Dads and supporter of other family-related organizations and ministries might be diminished because of what might be perceived as a parental failure. But his thoughts turned to the Bible story of Job—a man who was above reproach yet suffered through some of the most tragic sets of circumstances ever recorded.

As described in the biblical book, Satan asked God to remove His hand of protection from Job. It was Satan's belief that if Job were to suffer great misfortune, he would ultimately curse God. Satan proceeded to destroy everything of value in Job's life. Job certainly questioned God during this time of tribulation, but much to Satan's surprise and dismay, Job never turned his back on the Lord. Ultimately, God blessed Job for his faithfulness, not just by restoring his life, but also by giving him back twice as much as he had lost.

Dungy's personal loss may not have been as severe, but no doubt God has blessed him for staying faithful to the pursuit of integrity in the aftermath of such a devastating loss. The following season, in fact, Dungy experienced the pinnacle of success by leading the Colts to victory at Super Bowl XLI. In the process, he became the first African-American NFL coach to win the prestigious game.

And if Dungy wasn't already a beloved national figure, that single crowning achievement suddenly opened the floodgates for a whole new world of opportunity and influence. "That's the great thing about winning," Irsay says. "It gives you a stage. It gives you a podium where you can have a chance to demonstrate the virtues that are important to you."

Dungy agrees, but he warns that such a platform can also be treacherous to occupy if its foundation isn't cemented by one's commitment to integrity. And it's not about protecting an individual's image or salvaging self-respect and pride. Dungy says that his desire to live out integrity before others is rooted in a significant calling on his life, a calling that is shared by all who claim Jesus as their savior.

"It is very important for a Christian athlete or a Christian coach to model integrity," Dungy says. "Because once I have gone out there and said, 'I am a Christian—here are the principles I live by,' if I do anything that undermines that, that's hurting the cause of Christ, that's hurting the gospel. It would be better off for me not to say anything.

But once people know I am a Christian, I can't afford to walk differently than I believe because everybody is going to see, especially in a high-profile position like a college coach, a high-school coach, a professional coach. Eyes are on you all the time."

It's a scenario that brings to mind another image of Job—when his so-called friends criticized him and searched for the sins and failures that must have led to such devastating circumstances. But Dungy knows well that judgment and opposition can come even during the good times. In November 2004, *Monday Night Football* aired a racy pre-game skit in which Terrell Owens (then with the Philadelphia Eagles) costarred with *Desperate Housewives* actress Nicollette Sheridan. Dungy made a point to publicly denounce the skit for its immoral content, but his complaint was taken out of context when he mentioned his disappointment in Owens for furthering negative stereotypes about black athletes and sexual conduct.

In those moments, Dungy has been able to take his lead from the example of Jesus Christ, who during His ministry on Earth was constantly challenged by the religious leaders of the day—in particular the Pharisees—for teachings that shook the foundations of popular belief.

But unlike Jesus, who was a sinless and perfect man, Dungy quickly owns up to the reality of his own imperfections. In those times when he does make a mistake, he is all too aware of the ramifications—especially for the follower of Christ.

"It's really tough," Dungy admits. "It's tough on me when I don't follow through with what I say I'm going to do or if I do something different or something that I know is wrong. It's really hurtful, because I know that eventually that's going to come to light and not only make my job tougher, but more than that, it's going to cause people to question what Christianity is about."

And because of this honest recognition of his own humanity, Dungy finds it much easier to forgive and forget the trespasses of others around him. "I have a tendency to forgive people because that's what Christ is all about," Dungy says. "I've worked in situations where once you lose that integrity from your boss, you don't really look at them the same way; and you're still going to go out there and give it everything you've got, but something's a little bit different, and I don't want that to happen for me and the people I work with."

As the punter for Indianapolis, Hunter Smith has seen firsthand the disciplined but gentle manner in which Dungy handles problems that arise within the team setting. It's an approach that he says stands out in the rough-and-tumble world of the NFL.

"In a profession that is full of reactions, Coach Dungy has chosen to be a responder, and he responds as Christ would respond," Smith says. "Jesus didn't react to the people who came against Him; He responded to them in love, humility and justice. That's how I feel Coach Dungy runs his family, his team and his life."

Not surprisingly, Dungy's strong convictions regarding forgiveness and compassion—even for those who have failed to maintain a high level of integrity—are based first and foremost on the example set by Christ. It is Christ's unwavering consistency, described in all four Gospels, that challenges Dungy to live in a similar manner before his family, his team and the general public.

And despite the culture's growing amorality and indifference, Dungy holds firm to his belief that character still matters and that following Jesus' consistent model of integrity is the only way to maintain a clean reputation before men and, more importantly, before God.

"We have so many pressures coming at us that tempt us not to live up to our integrity," Dungy says. "It's so easy to say nowadays, 'Well, everybody else is doing it,' or to think it's not important to be 100 percent accurate and honest and truthful because, after all, winning is the most important thing. We're under that pressure, but you know what? My integrity is first, and it doesn't matter if we win or not. I'm not going to let anything jeopardize my integrity."

TRAINING TIME

1. Tony Dungy says that integrity is "what's inside of you." Describe a critical situation in which your character was brought to the forefront. Were you pleased or displeased by how you reacted?

2. Dungy has experienced the highest highs and the lowest lows, but people have always noted his consistent integrity. Do you find it easier to maintain integrity when things are going well or when things are going poorly?

3. Dungy says, "It's tough on me when I don't follow through with what I say I'm going to do or if I do something . . . that I know is wrong." How do you feel when you break commitments or make mistakes? What kind of effects do those actions have on your integrity?

4. Read Hebrews 13:7-8. What advice is given in this passage? Who are some spiritual leaders that you look up to as an example of integrity? What can you learn about integrity through the life of Jesus?

5. Francis Bacon once said that it's "not what we profess but what we practice that gives us integrity." What are some examples of talking the talk but not walking the walk? How important is it to practice integrity and not just profess it? How might the practice of integrity help with consistency?

"As a coach and dealing with my players, integrity is the most important thing. What they see from me, they can get that all the time. Whatever I say to them, they can count on it. If all of a sudden I'm telling them about a technique we're going to use on the field or that this is the right way to do things or if I tell them something about my personal life and I don't follow up on that, how can they believe anything that I'm trying to teach them? To have that trust factor and have them follow me as the leader, they've got to believe in me; and they can't have that shaken because what I say is different than what I do, or I say something one day and come back the next day and say something different. I think integrity goes hand in hand with trust. You can't have a good player-coach relationship without trust. You can't have a good staff relationship without trust. . . . [Integrity at home is] really the same thing, but it just carries over to your family, to your kids, to your neighbors, to everybody who comes into contact with you at home. Am I saying to my family, 'This is what I want you to do,' but I don't necessarily do them? Am I saying, 'This is what we're going to be all about as a family,' but maybe next week it won't be? I think that's very confusing."

—Tony Dungy

2

WITNESS PROTECTION
Shaun Alexander
NFL Running Back

Likewise, encourage the young men to be sensible about everything.
Set an example of good works yourself, with integrity and dignity in
your teaching. Your message is to be sound beyond reproach, so that the
opponent will be ashamed, having nothing bad to say about us.
TITUS 2:6-8

Live so that your friends can defend you but never have to.
ARNOLD H. GLASOW

For individuals striving to live with integrity, honesty is always the best policy. But some people will argue that oftentimes it's better to say nothing rather than allow the harsh truth to be spoken. Shaun Alexander is one of those people who err on the side of caution when it comes to the words he speaks.

That wasn't always the case for the Seattle Seahawks' running back. In fact, it wasn't long ago that Alexander would answer every question posed to him by the media with brutal honesty, regardless of what kind of fallout his response might cause.

"I'm a blunt person," Alexander admits. "I try not to beat around the bush; and when it comes to me, I'm just really open. I don't try to hide anything, because I think as soon as you hide something, it can be dangerous for anybody else. I just think that lying is a form of wickedness. I never want to get into that or half-truths. Those can be very dangerous things. That's why I'm blunt about things that I'm doing."

In 2004, Alexander learned a hard lesson about honesty. After the final game of the season against Atlanta, he finished one yard shy of the NFL rushing title but easily could have reached the mark had he been given one last attempt.

Afterward, a reporter asked him this loaded question: "How would you feel if Coach [Mike] Holmgren knew you were only one yard short and didn't give you the ball?" To that, Alexander responded, "Oh man, I would feel like I was stabbed in the back."

The comment, according to Alexander, was blown out of proportion, and "suddenly that turned into something crazy." The next thing he knew, the media was reporting a riff between Alexander and Holmgren, even though the two had previously enjoyed a close relationship (both are committed Christians) in Seattle—a relationship that remains strong to this day.

Alexander would later explain that he never really believed that Holmgren would purposely deny him the title, but the usually verbose Pro Bowl back made the decision to be more careful with his words and, if necessary, even resort to saying, "No comment," in a situation where honesty might not be understood or well received.

"Satan's biggest scheme is always to get the world to view you one way when you're really something else," Alexander says. "If you take the one-yard-short incident, then that makes it look like I'm talking about stats and trying to get the extra yard and winning awards. In reality, for me, I was talking about my relationship with Coach Holmgren. That was one of those things where God says we should pay attention and beware of the things you do and say. That's all throughout the Bible."

The situation initially proved difficult for Alexander, who has spent most of his life pursuing integrity. Even from a very early age, he has understood the meaning of good, moral character—thanks to the strong influence of his mother, who he speaks glowingly of throughout the pages of his 2006 autobiography, *Touch-down Alexander*.

"I'm from Kentucky, so I have one of those mommas that forced you to live a life that wasn't going to embarrass your family," Alexander jokes. "I didn't understand what it meant to embarrass God or not living to a Godly standard until later. But there was an uncompromising plan for life that we had to live by. You weren't cheating on your tests. You weren't stealing. Those things were instilled in me by my mom."

Later on in life, Alexander says he was blessed to have several people who bolstered the example that was set by his mother. His athletic career was especially ripe with true models of integrity and godly character. "I had some great high-school coaches that were men of integrity," Alexander says. "I think about my quarterback coach, Paul Gray, who actually worked for FCA. I value marriage a lot, and my parents got divorced when I was in sixth grade. So I just valued the way he looked at his wife compared to other women that were around. Those were the things I noticed."

At the University of Alabama, Alexander again was surrounded by coaches who showed him it was possible to be successful in sports and still maintain a high level of integrity. He also recalls husband and wife Lee and Lucy Sellers, from Tuscaloosa, who were involved in his Sunday School class. These surrogate parents helped him start the process of building a bridge between moral character and biblical principles.

"They were a hard-working family of integrity," Alexander says. "Everything was about taking the steps to get closer to God. You could see in their children that it's the way they lived. Those were people of integrity whom I just admired."

According to Alexander, his early pursuit of integrity was based on a basic desire to be a decent, moral person. He had a form of integrity in him but didn't understand that there was a calling attached to those who have accepted Jesus Christ as their Savior. Still, as a youngster, there was something different about him that pushed him away from typical childhood behaviors.

"You know, it's funny," Alexander recalls. "I tell everybody that I was saved at the age of 10. I remember I wanted to accept Jesus. I wanted to be different. I wanted to know about this Jesus Christ and live for Him. So I had some things in me. I remember being in a little penny store with some kids; and everybody was saying, 'Hey, let's go steal some jawbreakers.' And I just couldn't do it. I didn't know that I had a spirit of integrity. But there were just things in me that were like that."

That same attitude carried over into high school and college, where, despite being a popular athlete, Alexander committed to a life of purity. He saved himself until marriage, but admits it wasn't until later in his college career that he put such acts of integrity into their proper spiritual context.

"The summer before my junior year in college was the first year I worked at an FCA camp," Alexander remembers. "Before that, I didn't know that there were other guys out there like me. So I met some kids from all over the country, and we talked about integrity issues: How far is too far with drinking? How far is too far with girls? How far is too far with your language?"

Those kinds of intense discussions ultimately led him to 1 Peter 1:15-16, which showed him that a call to holy living is an important part of following Jesus.

"And then the question about integrity isn't, 'How far is too far?'" Alexander says. "It's 'Why not holy? Why not purity? Why not 100 percent?' When you start looking at it that way, it's like, 'Whoa!' Because I was always a good kid growing up. No cussing. No drinking. No sex. But it never hit me that if God said, 'Be holy, because I'm holy,' then there is no line. There is no, 'How far is too far?'

"So there was a switch in my thinking, even though the grace of God never allowed me to go that direction. Yeah, there were temptations around me. I was an All-American as a freshman. But it just wasn't in me to say, 'Oh, I'm standing up for God because this is the godly way to do it.' I was more like, 'I just don't do that.' I guess the integrity factor was covered by God's grace, and it still is. But it wasn't until that junior year when I realized God had called me to be like this, and then I accepted the calling to be a servant. That's when I called Him my Lord. That's when my relationship with God went to another level."

When Alexander joined the NFL fraternity in 2000, he wasn't an instant star. In fact, it wasn't until starting running back Ricky Watters suffered injuries in 2001 that Alexander received his first crack at serious playing time. After a breakout season in 2004, he followed up with the greatest statistical year of his career in 2005. Alexander broke the single-season total touchdown record (28) and was named the 2005 NFL MVP. The Seahawks also reached Super Bowl XL, where they lost to the Pittsburgh Steelers.

But more important than the individual kudos, team successes and astronomical salary increases, Alexander says it's the platform for his faith in Jesus that means the most to him. He has used his NFL fame as a way to reach young people—particularly teenage guys. Alexander spends time mentoring kids and teaching them the truths behind such passages of Scripture as Joshua 1:7, which reminds us to "be strong and very courageous"; 2 Timothy 5:2, which teaches young men to treat "the younger women as sisters"; and Titus 2:6-7, which encourages "young men to be sensible about everything."

"Integrity is such a straight shot," Alexander says. "There's no counterfeit. There's no two ways of doing it. I always tell anyone who's listening, 'You can't say, "That's my one little sin," when it comes to integrity, because integrity crosses all boundaries. If you have integrity for God, that's who you are. You're a man of integrity.'"

Alexander doesn't shy away from tough issues either. One of his favorite Scriptures is James 2:10-11: "For whoever keeps the entire law, yet fails in one point, is guilty of [breaking it] all. For He who said, 'Do no commit adultery,' also said, 'Do not murder.' So if you do not commit adultery, but you do murder, you are a lawbreaker."

That Scripture reminds Alexander of an analogy that he and his cousin Dan Brown used frequently while working at FCA camps in college.

"It doesn't matter how big the jug of water is or how small the cup of water is," Alexander says. "It only takes a little bit of water to make the whole thing mud. Integrity says, 'I'm not going to accept a pinch of that dirt.' Every now and then we all get dirty because we're selfish, sinful people, but when you start accepting pinches of dirt, it really gets bad."

And then there are those moments, like the aforementioned one-yard-short incident, when people look for chinks in the armor and attempt to call one's integrity into question. There was perhaps no better example of this than the punishment Alexander endured throughout the 2007 season at the hands of the fans and the media. He broke his wrist in the first game of the regular season, and by the midway point was also suffering from bruised ribs, a faulty knee and back problems. He missed three games and produced the lowest statistical totals since his rookie season in 2000, when he was a backup. Alexander took shots from the media and was even jeered by his own fans. Of course, those same fans would cheer when he made a big play or scored a touchdown, proving just how double-minded and fickle they can be. But strangely, Alexander says it was never as bad as it looked on the surface.

"The boat was rocking that year," Alexander says. "It was craziness. People were booing and acting crazy. But spiritually, this was one of the most refreshing years I've ever had. I was at such a place of peace. I knew I couldn't do the things that I was used to being able to do physically. One whole side of my body was out. So for me it was like, 'God, I can't do this anymore.' And He was like, 'Well, if you no longer care about your stats, go have fun with Me.' And I was like, 'Wow! I can do that? I can play the game and not have to get 100 yards and two touchdowns and not feeling like I let somebody down?' I was freed up this year. It was a very blessed and freeing year for me."

It was also another learning experience for Alexander because he began to understand that it's not always up to us to defend our integrity. That's not to say there are never times believers should stand up for themselves, especially in those times when the attacks can hurt the credibility of their witness. But ultimately, it's up to God to protect His people from all accusations and all forms of slander.

"People are going to believe what they want to believe," Alexander says. "At the end of the day, I walk into my house with my family, and I pull them all closer to God; and there's joy in our house and there's peace in our house. I walk into my church. There's joy in my church and there's peace in our church. With the boys I mentor, there's joy and there's peace. Even on my team, there's joy and peace on my team."

Wherever Alexander has a strong influence on others—with his team, with his family, with the young men he mentors, or with the general public—one of the most important messages he shares deals with protecting integrity and guarding against things that might bring on the judgment of this world. That means being honest with oneself and avoiding the obvious pitfalls that vary from person to person.

"Everybody has to be real with themselves," Alexander says. "Guys are always like, 'Shaun, you're just so strong not to sleep with any of those girls in college.' But honestly, I'm not that strong. I just kept myself away from all of that. I'm probably weaker than most of those guys. But I was real with myself. I knew that if I went out, something was going to happen. To be a Christian, you have to be real with yourself, but a lot of times guys aren't."

But perhaps most importantly in this day and age of moral ambiguity and relative integrity, Alexander says everyone needs to know what to do when they make mistakes and have a lapse in their moral character. After all, there is no such thing as the perfect person.

"I always remind people that all of us fall short," Alexander says. "None of us is really good enough for God. If you're emotionally bruised from sinning, that's a good thing. I always worry about the ones that love Jesus; but when they sin, they just say, 'Well, He's going to forgive me.' There's no bruising there. I'm not saying you should feel convicted to the point where you want to jump off a building, but there should be this soreness that you let the King of kings down."

Alexander is careful to temper those words with the message of mercy and grace that pervades the Bible and is especially prominent throughout the Gospels of Jesus Christ. He is quick to quote 1 Peter 4:8, which reminds us that "love covers a multitude of sins," and John 12:47, in which Jesus tells us, "For I did not come to judge the world but to save the world."

"At the end of the day, most people who don't know Jesus, they have some form of insecurity or depression or anger that they can't fix," Alexander says. "So I'm like, 'Let God save you, heal you, free you from those things.' That's what's awesome about God. With Him, you can have a life of peace."

TRAINING TIME

1. Shaun Alexander shared a story in which a candid response allowed an opening for his integrity to be questioned. Can you describe other situations in which keeping quiet on an issue might be more appropriate than speaking your mind? Would you define that action as a lack of honesty or the use of wisdom?

2. Read 1 Peter 1:13-16. What advice does Peter give about maintaining integrity in verses 13-14? What can you find in those verses that might inspire you to be challenged? In what ways can you "be holy" as Jesus is holy?

3. Read Titus 2:6-8. What do you think Paul means when he encourages Titus to "be sensible about everything"? What is the importance of setting a good example and having a message that is "sound beyond reproach"?

4. Alexander says, "Every now and then we all get dirty because we're selfish, sinful people, but when you start accepting pinches of dirt, it really gets bad." How does that analogy translate into your quest for integrity? Read James 2:10-11. What does this Scripture tell you about the nature of sin and its effect on your character?

5. Read 1 Peter 4:8 and John 12:47. What do those Scriptures tell you about the power of God's grace in relation to sin? How do those truths help you deal with the times that you fall short of God's glory?

"I broke my hand in the first game [of the 2007 season]. I bruised some ribs by about the third or fourth game. I hurt my knee by the seventh or eighth game. So by the time we got to the middle of the season, I really couldn't walk that well or breathe that well. I only had one good hand, and my back was locking up. People were saying, 'Man, Shaun's running soft.' The natural instinct for any man is to try and defend who you are. But you have to remember that's what Satan does. Satan tries to damage your integrity. You have to be tough to stand up for God in our country. You've got to be tough spiritually to have integrity. You've got to be tough to live with purity. You've got to be tough to love people after they've wronged you. Because in this country, it's understood that it's okay to have an enemy. It's okay to want to fight back. But God says, 'Vengeance is Mine.' So then you have to decide if your belief is in the Lord or if your belief is in feeling better and getting back at someone. Those are just issues of integrity and knowing that God is God. So even when people are attacking me, I just want to forgive them. I'm a lover of people. I want them to see truth in that. I want my attitude to show them a peace that almost bothers them to the point where they want to know more about it."

—Shaun Alexander

FOLLOW THE LEADER

Les Steckel
Fellowship of Christian Athletes President and CEO

For the LORD gives wisdom; from His mouth come knowledge and understanding. He stores up success for the upright; He is a shield for those who live with integrity so that He may guard the paths of justice and protect the way of His loyal followers. Then you will understand righteousness, justice, and integrity—every good path. For wisdom will enter your mind, and knowledge will delight your heart.

PROVERBS 2:6-10

As the centuries pass, the evidence is accumulating that, measured by His effect on history, Jesus is the most influential life ever lived on this planet.

KENNETH SCOTT LATOURETTE

For centuries, mankind has debated this universal question: Are leaders born or are they made? In other words, do people come out of the womb with leadership skills built into their DNA? Or is it the process of life combined with the right environment and proper education and training that help people develop into leaders?

Depending on who is asked, the answer will likely be different, which most likely means that leaders arise in both ways. While some people are born with certain gifts and abilities that might give them an advantage when it comes to leadership, others are not so blessed at birth but instead work hard to overcome whatever obstacles and challenges stand in their way.

But no matter what the answer is, one thing is for certain: Integrity is something that *never* comes naturally. Living a life of integrity goes against human nature. Just watch any toddler, and it's plain to see that doing the right thing must be first taught and then learned and, most importantly, practiced and lived out. And even then, we must still guard ourselves against things that might challenge our integrity.

Les Steckel says that one of the biggest hurdles people face in their quest to have integrity is the temptation to cave in to social pressures due to a natural desire to be accepted. As a former NFL football coach with over 30 years of experience at the collegiate and professional level, he often felt like a lonely outsider as he strived to live out the admonition found in 1 Peter 2:9, which in the *King James Version* refers to followers of Christ as "a peculiar people."

"There's not a lot of free time in coaching, but when there is, some coaches will go out and do some things that might challenge your integrity," Steckel says. "If you don't go along with those social settings, you may get ostracized, but you feel like you don't have a relationship with them like the others do. . . . It's a life that's different. The Scripture says that we are to be peculiar. You certainly don't want to be perceived that way at times."

According to Steckel—who retired from coaching in 2005 to accept the position of president and CEO of the Fellowship of Christian Athletes—one of the biggest problems our nation is facing is an attack on the foundations of integrity. Basic moral values are being diminished, and many people believe that integrity is nothing more than a synonym for honesty. But Steckel believes it's so much more than that.

"I've always said integrity is weaving your private world together with your public world," he says. "I think a man's reputation is what other men think about him. A man's character is what God knows about him. So the reputation is from his public life, but character is from his private life. Only God knows our lives, and if we're all honest, we all have secret lives. It's being alert to that; and as you grow older, you become aware of that and you try to deal with it."

For Steckel, it's been a long journey that started in Whitehall, Pennsylvania. One of the most memorable lessons he ever learned took place while he was attending college at the University of Kansas. His family was hardly affluent, so to travel to and from school in Lawrence, Kansas, he would hitchhike.

"One day my mom came to me and said, 'When you get back to KU, you call us collect and you ask for yourself, and that way we'll know you arrived safely,'" Steckel recalls. "And my dad overheard it, and I thought he was going to blast both of us. He went ballistic and said, 'Don't you dare do that. Do you know how dishonest that is, cheating a phone company by fooling them like that?' I was petrified. So I knew that when I got back, I was going to have to pay 70 cents to make a three-minute call on the pay phone. That showed me that if you're going to be honest in the little things, you had better be honest in the big things."

Steckel's education intensified in 1968 when, following his graduation from Kansas, he joined the Marine Corps and then a year later served in Vietnam as an infantry officer. In 1972, he joined the Marine Corps Reserves and served part-time while balancing his coaching career before retiring as a colonel in 1999.

"Being a Marine and spending 30 years in the Marine Corps, I found that they have tremendous principles of discipline and work ethic and esprit de corps and teamwork and camaraderie," Steckel says. "And yet within the ranks, there are always people who, surprisingly, let you down. That's what is challenging for a Christian man who is trying to live a life of integrity but from time to time faces battles he can't handle. That's when pride becomes an issue; and when pride becomes an issue, we try to solve the problems and defeat the opponent by ourselves and not realize that, like the Scripture says [in 2 Corinthians 12:10], when we're weak, God is strong."

Early in his coaching career, Steckel spent time as an assistant at Colorado and Navy before making the leap to the NFL with San Francisco in 1978. He spent 1979 to 1983 as an assistant coach with the Minnesota Vikings before taking over as head coach in 1984. It was a short-lived experience, however, as he was fired following the Vikings' 3-13 season.

Up to that point, Steckel had already been involved in various ministries, including FCA for 12 years. But his understanding of what true integrity really should look like in the life of a Christian man didn't come into focus until 1985 when he joined head coach Raymond Berry's staff at New England. In that first season, the Patriots reached their first ever Super Bowl, which they eventually lost to a legendary Chicago Bears team that featured head coach Mike Ditka and star athletes Walter Payton, Richard Dent, Mike Singletary and Jim McMahon.

Despite the hugely successful season, however, it was Berry's quiet, unassuming witness that made the strongest and most lasting impact on Steckel's life.

"Raymond was the greatest Christian model I ever saw," Steckel says. "One thing I knew for sure: When Raymond said something, it was the truth. You never questioned it—ever. When you have models like that in your life, then you want to emulate them. When I saw Raymond, he had qualities of Jesus that were lived out every day."

Steckel takes Berry's life as a model of Jesus, and he compares the qualities he observed in Berry to the "fruit of the spirit" that Paul wrote about in Galatians 5:22-23. "I saw love from Raymond for his players, for his wife and for his children," he says. "He had the patience of Job, and it drove me crazy at times. He showed me tremendous peace. I've never seen a guy in such stressful moments show such signs of peace. He was very gentle. I was so used to other head coaches who were fire and brimstone, and Raymond's talks were so gentle and his peace came through loud and clear. He was kind to everyone. Even the custodians and the parking-lot attendants—he knew those people by their first name. And that was a model for me, so whenever I've gone different places, I've tried to do the same.

"He was faithful," Steckel continues. "I can remember the day of Super Bowl XX. I had this great creative idea to do something in our game plan. I ran to his hotel room down the hall, and there he was in his robe reading his Bible the morning of the Super Bowl. I just thought, *Wow*. That made a real impact on me. And he showed great goodness to everyone."

In short, Berry modeled Christ to Steckel in a way that he had never quite seen before. And that up-close-and-personal viewpoint caused him to rethink the way he was modeling Christ to others around himself. But it wasn't until 1990 that Steckel fully understood what integrity was really all about. At that point, he found himself unemployed after a one-year stint at Brown University. In his autobiography, *One Yard Short: Turning Your Defeats into*

Victories, he describes in detail a 13-month period when God shattered him emotionally and spiritually, and then methodically pieced his life back together again.

"Prior to my brokenness in 1990, I'm not sure how much modeling I was doing," Steckel says. "I was doing a lot of talking. Without a doubt, after my brokenness, not only did I want to be an FCA guy, I wanted to model Christ and let people know that's who I was following. And I found it to be a very lonely life. There were times that I would walk into the locker room and there would be an instant hush. It wasn't so much that they were talking about me. They were saying things that they knew they shouldn't be saying, and I happened to be around. It was tough at times, but I tried to live out my priorities. I think a man of integrity needs to know what his priorities are."

"I've always said that my faith came first, and that wasn't true prior to my brokenness," Steckel adds. "My god was football. It wasn't Jesus Christ. But after my brokenness, it certainly changed quickly."

To remind himself of his renewed commitment to Christ-centered priorities, Steckel created a seven-point list that relies on a heavy dose of alliteration: (1) faith, (2) family, (3) football (since replaced by FCA), (4) friends, (5) fitness, (6) finances, and (7) fun.

"When I have to make a decision, I try to be a man of integrity, and I look at my priority list," Steckel says. "I ask myself, *Are you in fact living out your priorities?* and *Are you modeling Christ?*"

One of Steckel's new life verses is found in Proverbs 2:6-10, where Solomon talks about the kind of wisdom that comes only from God and was lived out through Jesus as portrayed in the Gospels. Steckel now had the original template that he needed to walk with divinely inspired integrity that will "guard the paths of justice and protect the way of [God's] loyal followers" (v. 8).

"We have this tremendous integrity modeled that we should try to emulate," Steckel says. "It's hard to emulate when you're not in the Word. So you don't really know who Jesus is except what people tell you. But the more you read about this living Son of God, you understand that integrity is a special character quality that so many people are labeled having. But do we have Christlike integrity? If you can't emulate the values you believe in, then you're obviously going to have a hard time getting other people to follow you along those lines."

Steckel spent two seasons at Colorado as an assistant coach under Promise Keepers' founder Bill McCartney before returning to the NFL, where he spent time at Denver, Houston, Tennessee, Tampa Bay and Buffalo. He was able to work alongside such solid Christian head coaches as Jeff Fisher and Tony Dungy. He also enjoyed the opportunity to coach in a second Super Bowl, but his Tennessee Titans lost to the St. Louis Rams in one of the NFL's most exciting championship games.

Still, with a greater commitment to integrity and more accountability support than ever before, Steckel absolutely

45

understood—as he continues to understand today—that he would need to be ready for any attacks that might come against his moral character.

"As a Christian, every day we take the playing field or, to use a military term, we take the battlefield," Steckel says. "If I'm aware of the enemy and what the situation is and who the enemy is, I've got a chance of winning the battles. Every day I wake up, it says in Ephesians I need to put on the armor of Christ—the helmet of salvation, the breastplate of righteousness, the belt of truth, the sandals of a peacemaker, the shield of faith and the sword of the Spirit. If you get out of your bed or out of the rack, as they say in the Marine Corps, without putting on the armor of Christ, you're going to get beat every day."

Once that armor has been donned, Steckel says the believer must then be able to recognize who the enemy is and learn how to fight against the attacks that are certain to come. Those attacks come in three progressively dangerous forms.

"First, there's the secular world," Steckel says. "All you've got to do is listen to people talk, watch television, watch people's actions and the next thing you know the secular world is dictating to you how to act. That's not what God wants us to do. Then there's selfishness. That's the biggest battle that we'll have all our lives, until we crawl into the grave. God talks about that all the time. I share that with my children. If you really want to have a fruitful, exciting Christian experience, you literally have to be totally empty of yourself and fill your life up with the spirit of the living God."

To combat those two enemies of integrity, Steckel recommends a healthy dose of Jesus' admonition in Luke 9:23: "If anyone wants to come with Me, he must deny himself, take up his cross daily, and follow Me."

But when Steckel brings up the third enemy of integrity, he admits that it sometimes draws some strange responses. "I know there are people out there who hear the term 'Satan' and think, *What are you making this up for?*" Steckel says. "But I can tell you that since I've been called to this position with FCA, I have been more aware of Satan than ever before in my life. There's really a battle. He does not want success to take place. And when he sees it, he just comes at you harder."

So when the temptation to cut corners or take the easy road makes its sly, sneaky entrance—and it assuredly will—Steckel reminds himself and advises others to consider Christ, the ultimate role model of integrity, and how He handled Himself in the face of death itself (see Matthew 26:39).

"There's no greater example of that than Jesus' going to the cross," Steckel says. "He knew that's what He was supposed to do. He had no desire to do it. He cried out to the Lord. But when it gets right down to it, you can have a clear conscience when you know you're living a life of integrity."

TRAINING TIME

1. Read Matthew 7:13-14. How would you compare the choice between the wide road and the narrow road to today's life choices? Why do you think so many take the path of destruction and so few take the road that leads to eternal life?

2. Read 1 Peter 2:9. What does this verse tell you about the kind of life to which Christians have been called? What are some pressures you have personally faced?

3. Steckel calls former New England Patriots head coach Raymond Berry "the greatest Christian model" he has ever known. Read Galatians 5:22-23. What are the "fruits of the spirit" in this passage? How might each one help you in your quest for a life of integrity?

4. When Steckel was offensive coordinator with the Tennessee Titans, he once made the choice to take the responsibility for a poor decision (see the "In His Own Words" section). Can you describe a time when you were faced with a similar decision? How did you ultimately react? How did that action affect your decisions from that point forward?

5. Read Proverbs 2:6-10. Who does this passage suggest is the perfect example of integrity? What are some of God's attributes (as exemplified by Christ) by which you should live?

"When I was offensive coordinator for Tennessee, we played the Steelers in Pittsburgh. On Saturday morning, another coach came to me and said, 'If we use this particular formation with this protection and they run this particular blitz, Steve McNair could get blindsided.' My immediate response was, 'They don't run that blitz, so why worry about it?' Sure enough, Pittsburgh was leading, and we were down by two scores; and we were on about the 15-yard line, and we're getting ready to go in and score. We lined up in what I referred to as a maximum protection, and wouldn't you believe it, they ran that blitz and hit Steve in the back. The ball bounced out of his hand, and one of the Steelers picked it up and ran 85 yards. I can remember that Monday at the team meeting, [head coach] Jeff [Fisher] was going over some of the events of the game. I stood up and said, 'Coach Fisher, can I share something with the team?' And I said, 'You know, oftentimes when we lose, nobody wants to take the blame, and they want to point their finger in the other direction. But everybody can point the finger at me.' I'll always remember that day because the players now had confidence in me, because they knew I was just as willing to call myself out in front of them as I was to call them out in front of other players when they made a mistake."

—Les Steckel

4

THE GUILT-FREE LIFE

Wendy Ward
LPGA Golfer

I always do my best to have a clear conscience toward God and men.
ACTS 24:16

The Bible is very clear: Don't do your good works before men to be cheered by men. . . . I do the right things because that's what God told us to do.
DAVID ROBINSON

Wendy Ward doesn't know how it happened. All that matters is that she knows it did. She didn't see her golf ball move, but when she realized that her putt no longer lined up, it was clear that the ball had rotated a mere "dimple or two." Ward had already grounded her putter, and she immediately knew that the sometimes unforgiving rules of the game were about to cost her a stroke.

But this wasn't just another average day at an average LPGA tournament. Ward was in the final group playing in the fourth and final round of the 2000 McDonald's LPGA Championship at the DuPont Country Club in Wilmington, Delaware. She had entered the day in a tie for the lead with legendary golfer Juli Inkster.

And there Ward stood on the green of the par-3 thirteenth hole, shaking her head at what had just occurred. But one thing that never crossed her mind was the possibility that no one else had seen what she had seen. Strangely enough, Ward would later learn that no one else had seen that the ball had moved, and she very well could have played on without penalty.

"There wasn't a decision," Ward remembers. "It was just a reaction. I didn't weigh the costs of whether or not I'd ever be in that position again for a major championship."

For Ward, her choice to follow the letter of golf's stringent law wasn't something that had just happened. The determination to say yes to integrity—hence turning away from the temptation to cheat—had been instilled in her character years earlier as a young girl being raised in San Antonio, Texas. Ward's father was a military man and subsequently lived by a strict honor code. Her mother was equally dedicated to showing their children a strong example of biblical morality.

"My folks strike me as the biggest example [of integrity]—from a simple lesson of telling the truth," Ward says. "They taught me you can hold true to your commitments and be honest about them, but you don't need to make excuses and go do something else. They always set that example of being honest with us and being honest with other people. There was no other option to telling the truth."

By the time Ward was seven years old, she was on her way to major success on the golf course. Her family would play together on the weekends—even on Sundays, immediately following their church's early service. And the lessons that she learned in her home always found a way into a game that also has a long-standing tradition of integrity and honesty.

"If I wasn't playing with my family on Saturdays or Sundays, I would be out on the golf course by myself," Ward says. "I would play two balls, and I'd play one against the other; and there wasn't any cheating. I was a very competitive person by nature. I guess in my household, rules were rules, and they weren't meant to be broken. There was a reason that they were in place, and I just respected that."

Despite attending church, reading parts of the Bible and knowing the story of Jesus, Ward had not taken that necessary step of making Him the Lord of her life. In the meantime, Ward was having a hugely successful amateur golf career, including winning the 1992 Texas State Women's title. She then left home to play for the perennial women's golf powerhouse at Arizona State University, where she was part of three NCAA championship teams (1993-95) and individually finished as the runner-up twice and in third place one time. Ward was also a three-time First Team All-American.

But during her sophomore year, Ward says she found herself struggling with college life in general. Her grades weren't as good as she wanted them to be, and her attitude toward golf was also taking a sharp turn in the wrong direction. Ward recalls one day talking on the phone to her golf instructor, Lori Brock, who had likewise noticed the negative changes in her pupil and asked if she had ever thought about attending ASU's Fellowship of Christian Athletes meetings.

"It's funny, because it's one of those critical moments where if your folks told you that, you probably would have closed the door," Ward says. "If my college coach would have said something, I would have been defensive. But because I had this admiration for my instructor, I said, 'You know, I'll check into that.'"

Ward approached Arizona State's head coach, Linda Vollstedt, and had already assumed she would say no because of a conflict between when FCA met and study hall. But without missing a beat, Vollstedt gave her star golfer permission to add the ministry to her college experience.

Ward likens her first FCA experience to "going to a new school." Even though the room was full of athletes, she didn't know any of them personally. But Ward was attracted to the environment created by the music that was already playing when she walked through the door. She had grown up in a church where her dad played the organ, and both of her parents were in the choir. Ward herself enjoys playing piano and was surprised to see one of the coaches playing guitar and leading the group in worship choruses.

"All of the sudden, the music mellowed me out," Ward says. "Any chip on my shoulder I might have had, I left at the door. They were singing songs that I didn't even know, and I was kind of getting into them. It was just that warm fuzzy feeling. You don't know where it's coming from, but it's something good. When I walked out of that room, I had this warm fuzzy feeling . . . but I also had this great feeling of jealousy. The reason I call it great is because I said, *These people have something I don't have. And I want it.* I went to my dorm and I was just overwhelmed, and I feel like that's when I truly accepted Christ as my Savior."

From that point on, things immediately began to change for Ward. Her attitude took a drastic turn for the better, and that played a significant role in the improvement of her performances on the golf course and in the classroom. Ward also says it was her newfound relationship with God that helped her understand the why behind her parents' faithful commitment to integrity.

"It comes at that point where you make a commitment to follow and walk with Christ," Ward says. "Then you basically start reading the Word and find out things that you must uphold to call yourself a Christian. I don't want to bring shame to His name, because I'm placed on Earth only to glorify His name. Anything short of that is displeasing to Him."

After graduating from Arizona State in 1995 with a degree in business management, Ward turned professional that summer and competed in four LPGA events. She qualified for the tour on her first try and debuted as a rookie in the 1996 season. A year later, she won her first tournament by topping the field at the 1997 Fieldcrest Cannon Classic. Ward's sudden-death playoff victory at the 1998 Cup Noodles Hawaiian Ladies Open not only gave her a second career title but also solidified her standing as one of the rising stars on the tour.

But as Ward took the thirteenth green on the final day of the 2000 LPGA Championship, she was looking to break a drought that was nearing two years in length. As she stared down at that displaced golf ball, the ramification of what taking an extra stroke might have on her chances of winning was the furthest thing from her mind.

"When that ball moved, I didn't think twice," Ward says. "In fact, when I saw it move, I thought that the whole world saw it. When you're in the last group on Sunday, the cameras are rolling, and the gallery is around the green. I stepped back and thought, *You've got to be kidding me.* I remember looking up to my playing partner and good friend Juli Inkster, and she looks at me and she's like, 'What?' And I said, 'The ball moved. Did you see it?' And she's like, 'No.' It never crossed my mind, *Oh, I wonder if anybody else saw it.* I didn't think of the consequences. I didn't think about how it was going to make me look. I come to look at it now and see that it was the closest that I ever got to winning a major, and yet the platform that God put me on was so much greater."

At the end of the day, Ward can't say for sure that the stroke cost her the tournament, but it is clear that doing the right thing cost her a shot at the resulting playoff.

Instead, Ward—who finished in a tie for third place— watched from the clubhouse to see the final result. What happened after that was a remarkable moment that completely took Ward by surprise.

"Juli Inkster went on to win that tournament, and the top three people have to attend the award ceremony," Ward recalls. "We got up on the green, and she was giving her speech, and she said, 'I'd love to stand here and sing praises about how great I played today, but I have to give credit to Wendy because she's the true champion today.' I wasn't expecting that. She was still trying to figure out, 'Are you sure the ball moved?' She felt like she'd been gifted the trophy, and she felt like what I did was more of an example and a victory for the game of golf. To this day, when we stumble across that story, she'll still tell me, 'I don't think that ball moved.' Yet I know it did. I didn't make it move, but that doesn't matter. It's just the rule."

Ward admits that even the kind words by Inkster were not enough to console her from the heady reality that she had come so close to a major championship.

"I was pretty deflated at the end of the day," Ward admits. "It's funny, because I didn't feel like I lost the tournament due to that one stroke. I felt like I had lost the tournament because my chipping was horrendous that week. So I was talking to my instructor that evening on the phone about how my short game had abandoned me, and he kept going back to, 'Are you sure that ball moved?'"

"I wasn't proud that it happened," Ward adds. "I was mad for a time at God for letting it happen. I was like, 'How could You let that ball move?' Then I realized that there was a greater lesson there. It took a few days for it to really sink in what I had given up, or what I had lost. But then what I had truly gained and the reason that I'm out there playing and the concept of the audience of One really came into play for me. We play for an audience of One."

A year later, Ward broke her winless streak by claiming the 2001 Wendy's Championship for Children. Her fourth and most recent tournament victory came in 2005 at the LPGA Takefuji Classic. Ward's other achievements since 2000 consist of numerous top 10 finishes and membership on three U.S. Solheim Cup teams—including the championship squad in 2005.

With just over $3.5 million in career winnings, Ward understands the temptation that some may face when it comes to similar situations such as the one she experienced that day. She estimates that finishing tied for third instead of possibly winning the tournament most likely resulted in a $120,000 pay cut.

When other golfers are faced with the same choice, Ward has often watched them make the selfish choice that slowly but surely begins to chip away at their integrity. "It's funny, because there have been a few situations where that has happened; and different players have claimed that they didn't ground their putter, yet TV shows that they did," Ward says. "That's when my stomach turns, because it's not the right thing to do. I don't know how somebody could go on, but again it's just a difference in where you stand in your heart and your mind."

Ward has yet to repeat her near-miss championship run from the 2000 season, but the blessings she received from choosing integrity that day have been plentiful—maybe not so much in terms of financial gain or personal accolades, but certainly in the way her stand has touched the lives of those who were watching from a distance.

"The neatest thing was when I would have a dad come up to me at a tournament a month or so later with his little daughter," Ward says, "and he would say, 'Hey, I know you don't want to revisit this, but I told my daughter about what happened a month ago, and she really thinks it is cool that you were that honest. That was a really neat lesson that I got to share with her, and you're her favorite now.' And I got a lot of fan mail about it."

Ward's deep-seated understanding of the importance of integrity, instilled in her by her parents, had been convicted by her years of studying the virtues of Jesus Christ. Jesus Himself was once tempted to compromise His integrity, a story that can be found in Matthew 4:1-11. While nearing the end of a 40-day fast in the wilderness, Jesus was approached by Satan who on two separate occasions tried to talk the Son of God into performing miraculous feats in order to prove His divine identity. During a third confrontation, Satan tempted Jesus to bow down to him in exchange for "all the kingdoms of the world" (v. 8).

Every time Satan came to Jesus, the Savior rebuked him by quoting God's Word. There wasn't a long thought-out process. He didn't take time to go and ask a friend for advice. Jesus simply did the right thing, because He knew that even though no man would ever see His actions that day, God in heaven was watching. Jesus was keenly aware of that fact, and the thought of denying His Father undoubtedly never crossed His mind.

And while Ward admits she has made her fair share of mistakes, one thing that truly gives her joy is the knowledge that when push comes to shove, she knows that she will always do right by her relationship with God when it comes to matters of integrity, honesty and character.

"Our success each year is measured by where you finished on the money list," Ward explains. "The world creates that scenario and that standard. But God calls us to measure ourselves against His standards, His rules. I try to just play for Him, play for His approval. Can I walk off the course each day knowing, number one, that I gave my best; number two, that I didn't give up; and, number three, did my actions and attitude uphold everything that I stand for? Will He be pleased with me at the end of the day?"

TRAINING TIME

1. Wendy Ward had the opportunity to cheat but chose not to do so. Have you ever been tempted to gain a competitive advantage by breaking the rules? If so, what happened? Did you find it easy or difficult to make that choice? How did you feel after the fact?

2. Read Matthew 4:1-11. What are some of the ways Jesus was tempted? What defense mechanisms did He use to ward off Satan's temptations? How can you apply Jesus' methods to your life?

3. Ward's story of integrity gave her a greater platform to share her faith. In what ways can a lack of integrity impede a person's opportunity to share the gospel?

4. What do you think Ward means when she says she plays "for an audience of One"? How does buying into that belief make a difference when it comes to making difficult choices that might affect integrity?

5. Read Acts 24:16. What do you think it means to "have a clear conscience toward God and men"? Can you describe the difference between having a clear conscience versus a guilty conscience? What might be some of the benefits of having a clear conscience? What things do you do personally in order to maintain a clear conscience?

"I had hit my shot up there, and I marked it. It was getting late in the day, so the greens were getting dried out and a little crusty. I had a real distinct way that I placed my ball down at that time. A lot of girls do it. I used the writing on the ball to line up the intended line I wanted the ball to roll on. I also had a line in the middle of my putter, so it made a lot of sense. I had read the putt, and I had placed the ball and I set my putter down so my lines were perfectly in sync. I only had about an eight-foot putt. I looked away and when I looked back, the ball had rotated towards me, so my lines no longer matched up. That's when I backed off. I mean, we're only talking a dimple or two. I mean, it wasn't much. It's funny, because I could sit here and question myself forever; but at that time that was the technique that I used to line up my putt, so in my mind I couldn't even pull the trigger. That ball was no longer in the center of my club face, and it wasn't going on the line that I wanted it to. In a way, I almost feel like God had His hand on that—not only for the greater story, but He was protecting me. If there was any chance of me saying, 'Oh, I don't think anybody saw that,' He didn't even give me an opportunity to hit that ball, because in my own mind, I couldn't hit it because it wasn't even lined up right."

—Wendy Ward

5

LIVING AGAINST THE GRAIN

Bobby Jones
Former NBA Forward

---

*Do not be conformed to this age, but be transformed by the
renewing of your mind, so that you may discern what is the good,
pleasing, and perfect will of God.*

ROMANS 12:2

The time is always right to do what is right.

MARTIN LUTHER KING, JR.

Ask anyone associated with the American Basketball
Association (ABA) or the National Basketball Association
(NBA) throughout the mid to late '70s and the early '80s
about the hardest-working players in professional hoops
and inevitably one name will come up time and again:
Bobby Jones.

Legends such as Julius Erving, Charles Barkley, Larry
Brown and Dean Smith—men who all played alongside or
coached Jones—all give the same glowing praise of his
blue-collar work ethic, his respect for the game and its
rules, and his virtuous life of integrity.

One might imagine Jones as a kid shooting hundreds of free throws a day and then spending time reading the Bible after finishing his homework. That would make perfect sense, considering both the Christian walk and the hardworking attitude he displayed throughout a 12-year career that resulted in playing stints with the Denver Nuggets (1974 to 1978) and the Philadelphia 76ers (1978 to 1986). Plus, he was the son of Bob Jones and the younger brother of Kirby Jones, both of whom played college basketball at Oklahoma State University.

But strangely enough, Jones was never a stereotypical youth-group kid growing up. Furthermore, he was more like a couch potato than anything resembling the hustling, defensive specialist NBA fans grew to love and respect.

"I wasn't a Christian, but I grew up in church," Jones says. "They shared the gospel, and it went in one ear and out the other for me. It was my fault. It wasn't anybody else's. Really, I didn't have an interest in those spiritual things when I was younger. There wasn't much that interested me. I wasn't interested in sports. I would come home from school and sit around and get a bottle of pop and watch TV. It wasn't really until my dad pushed me to play sports that I started to develop those skills."

Jones was born in Akron, Ohio, but his father's work as a store manager for Goodyear Tires forced the family to make several moves, including stops in Bryan, Texas; New Orleans, Louisiana; Goldsboro, North Carolina; and Winston-Salem, North Carolina. By the time his family landed in Charlotte, North Carolina, he and his siblings were entering their formative years. He didn't realize it at the time, but he later understood how his father's next decision was one of great integrity.

"My dad refused to take anymore promotions if it meant moving the family," Jones says. "He understood that living like gypsies wasn't the best for family stability. I feel like he sacrificed his career advancement for our family. I think that the integrity of knowing that your responsibility is for your family more than your job he demonstrated by his actions."

Another influential man of character in Jones's life was former University of North Carolina head coach Dean Smith. Still considered one of the greatest college basketball minds of all time, Smith made a lasting impression on Jones from day one.

"Before the season, Coach Smith brought every freshman into his office for a talk," Jones says. "He said to me, 'Bobby, are you the kind of player who would respond to me screaming at you to motivate you, or would you just like me to correct what you're doing wrong?' And I was stunned that he would ask my opinion. So I responded to him as honestly as I could. I said, 'Well, coach, I would just appreciate it if you would just tell me what I'm doing wrong. I don't think I'm motivated by someone yelling at me.' For the next four years, he never yelled at me. Now there were other guys who told him they needed a kick in the rear sometimes, and he would do that. He would verbally get on those guys more. But the fact that he asked the question and stuck to that for the next four years is something I'll never forget."

Jones knew what integrity was when he saw it. And he definitely saw it in the living examples of his father and his college coach. But it wasn't until he accepted Christ in 1973, right before his senior year in college, that the concept of God-inspired integrity started to infiltrate his heart.

"I can't pinpoint a time where I first realized that I needed to be a man of integrity," Jones says. "I did know that as a Christian, I was called to live my life in a way that would honor Him. My prayer when I got saved was two things: (1) Forgive me of my sins, so I can live in heaven with You forever, and (2) Show me how to live as a Christian in a world that views Christians in a cockeyed way. I really feel like He allowed me to do that. He allowed me to let my yes be yes and my no be no."

A year earlier, Jones was in Munich, Germany, playing on the U.S. Olympic basketball team. It was the year of the notorious 1972 Summer Olympics, when terrorists held 11 Israeli athletes hostage. By the end of the intense stand-off, all of the Israeli athletes had been killed. Jones and his teammates assumed the Games would be cancelled, but that wasn't the case.

Instead, the heavily favored U.S. team competed and played its way into the gold-medal game against the former Soviet Union. With three seconds left, Doug Collins hit two free throws to give the Americans a one-point lead.

Then a bizarre set of circumstances resulted in three opportunities for the Soviet team to inbound the ball, even though the referees attempted to end the game after the Soviet team's first failed attempt to score. The referees were overruled by then International Amateur Basketball Federation secretary general R. William Jones of Great Britain, who came out of the stands to singlehandedly alter the outcome of the game. The result was a 50 to 49 victory for the U.S.S.R.

"We as a team decided not to accept the silver medal," Jones says. "I still stand by it. I believe it was the right decision. That was a point where the integrity of the people running the contest was really nonexistent. I think there is a time when you can protest, and you can react when things are not done according to law or rule or the right way; and I think we did that, and I think we did it appropriately."

After his junior year, Jones was drafted by the ABA's Carolina Cougars, but he decided to return to North Carolina for his senior season. In 1974, he was drafted by the NBA's Houston Rockets. The Cougars moved to St. Louis and became known as the Spirit of St. Louis but still had the ABA rights to Jones. Coach Larry Brown was with the ABA's Denver Nuggets and traded for him. Still needing to decide between the two competing leagues, Jones went with the former University of North Carolina coach and what he perceived as a better opportunity for immediate playing time.

At that point, Jones had only been a Christian for a year. Unsure of what challenges he was about to face, he was blessed with teammate Claude Terry, who had been a believer for several years. The two became good friends, roommates and Bible study partners. In the meantime, Jones quickly developed a reputation for playing the game with the highest level of integrity.

"For me it was always a situation where just because you're playing a game doesn't mean that as a Christian you can be dirty to a player or berate an official," Jones says. "You don't get a free pass because they're your so-called opponent. The Lord tells us to be good to our enemies; and by doing that, you throw coals on their head. But that also goes back to where you want to be that living example of a Christian."

Jones never got caught up in the common practice of trying to sell a call to the officials. He always felt like that was a cheap approach. Instead, Jones wanted to be a witness of integrity and faith to the referees and to his opponents. While he wasn't perfect in his attempt, Jones certainly was unique in his philosophy; and as his career continued, the referees began to place an unusual amount of trust in his well-documented character.

"It was one of the last years in my career, and we were playing down in San Antonio," Jones recalls. "The ball goes out of bounds, and I'm trying to save it. I blocked out the official's view, and he couldn't tell whether it went off my fingertips or not. So he goes to the stands and retrieves the ball; and he says to me out of the side of his mouth, 'Bobby, did you touch it?' And I was just stunned. I get to play, and here I get to ref too. And I was honest with him; and I said,

'No, I didn't touch it.' And he said, 'Okay, red ball.' So we got to inbound it right there."

"Now, this is how the Lord works," Jones continues. "Two weeks later, the exact same scenario takes place. It was the same ref, but this time it's in Philly, and it's right in front of our bench. The ball goes out of bounds again, and I'm going after it; and this time it does touch my fingertips. The ref comes up to me and says, 'Bobby, did you touch it?' And I said, 'Yeah.' And Coach [Billy] Cunningham was right there; and he kind of stamped his feet a little bit and says, 'Bobby, that's his job! Let him make the call!' I didn't respond to that, but I thought in my mind, *My integrity's not worth a possession.*"

Jones's integrity was perhaps even more noteworthy off the court, where from day one he refused to cave in to the lifestyle of debauchery that many professional athletes live.

"I never wanted to be a part of that lifestyle," Jones says. "The Bible taught me to be faithful to my wife and to avoid the appearance of evil. I've always been a homebody anyway. In high school, my idea of a big night out was to play board games with some buddies of mine. I was never a partier anyway; and then when I started playing pro ball, my style of play was such that I was so tired at the end of the game, I didn't feel like going out anyway. That was a non-factor for me as far as temptation or a distraction."

In fact, Jones says the toughest part of his NBA career was the travel that didn't allow him to attend Sunday church services during the season. During his career with the Philadelphia 76ers (where he won the Sixth Man Award and was part of the NBA Championship team in 1983), he benefited from personal Bible study meetings with his pastor every Tuesday. Just like his commitment to intense practice and on-court hustle, Jones was equally attuned to the need for consistent times of prayer and devotion.

While Jones has been away from the pro game for more than 20 years now, he can honestly say that not much has changed when it comes to integrity and our society. Some people may argue that there has been a steady decline in moral behavior during that time, but Jones simply believes that the decline of personal ethics has been ongoing since the fall of man.

"The world is what it is," Jones says. "Satan does have control of it. But the Lord does provide a comforter—the Holy Spirit—to give us that power to do the things we should in the right way. That doesn't mean that we're always going to be met with success. Negative things are going to happen. People are going to get fired. People are going to get berated. People are going to be made fun of because of their faith."

Even though he no longer enjoys the large platform that life in the NBA affords, Jones continues to do his part when it comes to telling others about Jesus and teaching people (in particular, teenagers) what it means to live a life of integrity.

In 2003, he joined forces with former NBA players Bart Kofoed and David Thompson to create 2XSALT, Inc.

Inspired by Matthew 5:13 ("You are the salt of the earth"), this ministry runs sports camps, clinics, leagues and an after-school program that mentors students. He is also the volunteer coach at Myers Park High School in Charlotte.

Jones uses those opportunities to share his personal definition of integrity and a philosophy that comes from years of real-life experience.

"Integrity is doing the right thing and not considering the consequences," he says. "It's simple to say; and really once you start doing it, it's kind of simple to live, when you trust that God's got His best for you."

That truth is fortified by one of Jones's favorite Scriptures, Romans 12:2, a well-known passage that implores believers not to "be conformed to this age, but be transformed by the renewing of your mind, so that you may discern what is the good, pleasing, and perfect will of God."

In a society where athletes are cheating to get a competitive advantage, politicians are bending rules to line their wallets, and corporations are ignoring basic ethics to pad the bottom line, Jones says our value systems have been irreparably damaged to the point that a lot of people believe it's okay to backstab or cut corners in order to be successful.

But Jones's prayer for this nation's youth—the next generation of leaders—is that they follow the examples of such Bible heroes as Daniel and the three young Hebrew men who refused to give in to the world's way of doing things and instead chose to live pure and holy before God.

"Daniel and his three buddies just lived their lives according to the way they knew they should live it, not according to their circumstances," Jones says. "That made it simple for them to make their decisions. It didn't make the decisions very pleasant, I'm sure at the time, but it gave them their groundwork and God's standard for their life. Those are the examples that we have. We can choose to follow those examples, or we can say, 'Hey look, everyone else is doing it. Why not?'"

Jones also hopes that young people will accept a challenge similar to the one given by Mordecai to Esther, the queen and divinely appointed rescuer of her people. In Esther 4:14, Mordecai suggested that she had been brought "to the kingdom for such a time as this."

"We've been placed where we are for a reason," Jones says. "That reason is to honor the Lord and to stand in the gap where there is a lack of integrity or where there is a lack of honesty or a lack of boldness for the gospel. I think a lot of kids want to be the superstar, but that's just not the way it is. I mean, half of my career, I came off the bench. It didn't really matter to me if I started a game. But there's a pride factor in there where we tend to gravitate to the slickest-talking pastor or the most popular kid in school, and that becomes our standard. Well, that's very temporary; and Scripture is there for a reason, and it has been proven true over thousands of years."

TRAINING TIME

1. Bobby Jones gives two personal examples of integrity: his father and Coach Dean Smith. How do those two examples go against the grain of the way today's society thinks?

2. How do you think having an established believer like Claude Terry as a teammate helped Jones? How important is accountability and Christian fellowship in your walk?

3. In Jones's story about the game in Cleveland (see the "In His Own Words" section), he tells about a letter written by a fan who was impressed by his Christian example on the court. What are some ways that you might be able to live against the grain in different areas of your life? How might that help you point others to Jesus?

4. Read Romans 12:2. What do you think it means to "be transformed by the renewing of your mind"? What are some tools that might help you accomplish that task?

5. Who are some modern-day examples of integrity who inspire you? Read Esther 4:14. How do you interpret the phrase "for such a time as this"? For what purpose do you think God might be calling you to live a life of integrity?

"I get letters every week from people asking me to sign basketball cards or something. They'll tell me that they saw me play a game and talk about the effort I gave. I met a guy about two years ago who told me a story about how he watched me play in Cleveland. The Cavaliers used to play out in the middle of nowhere. The arena was between Cleveland and Akron, and it was the most depressing place to go to in the dead of winter. We would go out there, and we'd always have bad games, because we didn't want to be there; and the bus drive out there was bad. It was just kind of a depressing place to play. Despite that, I always gave the effort I wanted to. So this guy relates this story to me. He was a Christian, and he wanted to take an unsaved friend to an NBA game to watch me play because he wanted to show this guy how a Christian plays. He said, 'You did that. You played as hard, if not harder, than anybody on the court.' That was a tool to allow him to witness to his friend about the Christian life. As a player, you don't even think about there being a guy in the stands who brought a guy to come see me play. I was by far not the star of the team. I was just part of a supporting cast to Julius [Erving] and Moses [Malone]."

—Bobby Jones

6

Temple Maintenance

Josh Davis
U.S. Gold Medalist in Swimming

Do you not know that your body is a sanctuary of the Holy Spirit who is in you, whom you have from God? You are not your own, for you were bought at a price; therefore glorify God in your body.

1 CORINTHIANS 6:19-20

Every man is the builder of a temple called his body.

HENRY DAVID THOREAU

Josh Davis is thankful for a lot of things. He's accomplished greatness as a world-class swimmer, winning a combined five Olympic medals (including three gold medals) and breaking American and world records. As a family man, he is a devoted husband and proud father of five children. Davis is also thankful to have a nice house and a big car that's spacious enough for the entire bunch. He even has had a building named after him—the Josh Davis Natatorium—in his hometown of San Antonio.

It certainly sounds great, but Davis will be the first to admit that everything on that list and more doesn't mean much without one key ingredient. "The most valuable thing I have, the most treasured asset I have, the thing I have to guard above everything else is my integrity, my character, my reputation," he says. "It is the most valuable thing I have."

The road that led Davis to that astute realization can be traced back to his strong ancestry—a family that moved to Texas in the late 1800s and has been there for the five generations ever since. Much of the groundwork for who he is today was laid long before he was born on September 1, 1972—ironically the same day that swimming legend Mark Spitz earned one of his seven gold medals at the Olympic Games in Munich, Germany.

"I've got a strong sense of identity rooted in my Irish heritage," Davis says. "It was fun for me to look back at my father, my grandfather, my great-grandfather and my many uncles and great-uncles and their involvement in the community as leaders and lawyers and speakers. So that's subconsciously been a factor in me figuring out what it means to be a man of integrity. I had a respect for going to church and a respect for spiritual things, but that's about as far as it went."

When Davis was 13 years old, he decided to take up swimming. The late start didn't afford him the best opportunity to succeed. His first coach, in fact, told him he should quit and switch sports. Davis made a change, but it was to get a new coach, not to leave the pool. From that point on, everything started to improve.

By the end of his freshman year, Davis was one of the best swimmers in the state for his age group. At the age of 15, just two years into his swimming career, he became a freestyle state champion. Davis repeated that feat the following year, and by the time that he was 17, he was the fastest swimmer in the country. That accomplishment opened the door to a full scholarship at the University of Texas, which has one of the most prestigious collegiate swimming programs in the country.

Davis says he was excited to go to college and gain the freedom that comes from life outside of the home. The sky was the limit, and he had the next four years of his life precisely mapped out.

"I was going to make good grades, swim real fast and if I had the time, I'd go to church," Davis says. "And then I was going to try to meet all 25,000 girls on the UT campus. Of course, I didn't have time for church. Swimming had become my god. When I was swimming good, I felt good. When I was swimming bad, I felt bad. My identity and my value came from my sport instead of God."

It didn't take long for Davis's poor choices to start catching up with him. He vividly remembers the toll that the stereotypical college life quickly took on him physically and emotionally. But even during his lowest moments, Davis now recognizes how God's grace and patience were present all along.

"Basically I was partying too hard and I got very, very ill at the end of my freshman year," Davis says. "God used that experience to bring me to a bottom-of-the-barrel moment where I had to look up. I explain it with good theology now. Some people say I found God. Well, God was never lost. I was the one who was lost. God gave me the strength and courage to respond to His truth.

"For the first time in my life, I realized that God created me. God knows how I best operate, so surely I can trust God with every area of my life. It seems so simple, but yet I think it flies over most people's heads, and we don't consult our Maker. We don't consult the playbook or the guidebook or the manufacturer's directions. I came to the point where I realized what I was doing with my life wasn't working. Even if I did want to do what was right, I don't think I had the power to do it anyway."

At the time, Davis didn't fully understand the spiritual dynamic at play. As is typical of the average college freshman, he was salivating at the chance for freedom from the regulations and responsibilities that come with parental guidance. Now, he could go where he wanted. He could eat what he wanted. He could do, really, whatever he wanted to do. As long as he went to class and made swim practice, Davis was his own man.

Instead, the star swimmer became enslaved to what he refers to as "the three *D*s of the freshman year." Davis was drinking too much, he was involved in dysfunctional relationships, and he was making bad decisions.

"Here I was this disciplined, straight-*A* student," he says. "I built up my résumé all through high school, but when I got to college and thought I had real freedom, I really didn't have it at all. I didn't have true freedom. True freedom is the ability to do the right thing when you want to do it, regardless of what anybody else is doing around you. I didn't have that and I needed that. I needed something more. I needed something outside of myself for wisdom and guidance and power to have true freedom."

At that point, Davis says he made Jesus his head coach; but, more importantly, he accepted Christ as his Savior, his Lord and his King. He also began diving into the Bible and gained a new perspective on life. One of Davis's favorite Scriptures is John 10:10, in which Jesus says, "I have come that they may have life and have it in abundance."

It didn't take long for Davis to acknowledge the need to study and memorize God's Word. The truth and relevance found within its pages were a source of power to which he had never before had access. And one of the first nuggets of wisdom that he learned was in Psalm 119:9: "How can a young man keep his way pure? By keeping Your word."

Another way Davis grew in his spiritual walk was through intense fellowship and accountability through various organizations, including Fellowship of Christian Athletes. "I got involved in FCA right away," Davis recalls. "I got involved in leadership and Bible studies, and I started going to church. In fact, during my sophomore year, I was involved in an FCA Bible study, a church Bible study and an AIA [Athletes in Action] Bible study. My grades weren't so good that year, but boy, I was soaking up the Word."

That commitment to devotion, prayer and community reaped a multitude of benefits. Davis learned how to share his faith; and, more importantly, he learned what it meant to be a man of integrity.

"Real men love Jesus," he says. "Real men are so filled with the love that Jesus has for them, they love God more than anything else in the world—more than the lust of the flesh like fame or pornography or being the life of the party. That's what integrity means to me, and really it's the essence of the Christian life. You fall more in love with God than anything else around you. All those things that the world has to offer seem kind of silly."

The next three years of his college career were completely different from the first. Davis's teammates thought that he had lost his mind. But had they been able to fast-forward and see the future, he is convinced they might have thought differently about the drastic changes that God took him through.

"They went on their way, messing around with a couple different girls a year and partying," Davis says. "Some of them figured it out and got married, and they're doing fine. But a lot of them aren't. A lot of them look old; and I wonder as they approach 40 if they're thinking, *Man, it would be nice to have a spouse or a family or maybe be a little further along in my vocation and my journey in life, but I'm not.*"

"I just feel very blessed," he adds. "I love having these five kids. I love my wife. I love that I've found a vocation that I really like. This is cool. I mean, all those decisions that seemed so weird and old-fashioned back then are producing a bountiful harvest now."

As Davis continued to study the Bible, he discovered further instructions on how to live a life of integrity. The apostle Paul's letter to the Ephesians became especially important in his quest for purity. Davis took to heart the teaching in Ephesians 4:29: "No rotten talk should come from your mouth."

"I realized the power of my words and that I needed to choose my words carefully and say only things that built people up," Davis says. "I didn't need to cuss anymore. I didn't need to gossip anymore. I didn't need to talk bad about people. Obviously a huge part of integrity is talking right."

Davis continued through Ephesians 5 and discovered that "sexual immorality and any impurity or greed should not even be heard of among you" (v. 3).

"I thought to myself, *Holy cow! I don't have a clue how to treat ladies*," Davis says. "*I don't have a clue how to find a life mate.* I had to do some serious business with God to figure out about courting and marriage and what it means to be a man in that way—preparing to be a husband and a father."

Another wake-up call came in the form of Ephesians 5:18, a Scripture that tells believers: "Don't get drunk with wine, which [leads to] reckless actions." Davis read that passage and suddenly realized that not only was his underage, heavy consumption of alcohol hindering his performance as a swimmer, but it was also against the law, not to mention physically destructive.

"Drinking is hard on your liver because your liver has to try to get that toxin out," Davis explains. "It puts stress on your digestive system. It slows down your nervous system. It is not a good thing. It does nothing for you. If you need that to meet people and to dance better, you're in a sad place."

Davis was eventually led to 1 Corinthians 6:19-20. These eye-opening verses showed him that the body of a follower of Christ "is a sanctuary of the Holy Spirit" (v. 19) and that his body should "glorify God" (v. 20). That's when Davis made the connection between worship and health. And while he says that he sometimes feels like the street-corner preacher whom the pedestrians try to ignore, nutritional science is becoming more popular as a natural performance-enhancing method.

"Athletes are realizing the benefits of nutritional science and are getting smarter," Davis says. "There are more good supplements available, good restaurants and those kinds of things. If they want it, it's out there. I still see plenty who don't have a clue. They have all of this genetic potential. They work so hard, yet they don't give themselves a chance to recover and build healthy cells outside of their training.

"I get excited, because when you eat right, drink lots of water and sleep a lot, I really believe you can almost stop the aging process. That's exciting to me. We're seeing people prove this in sports and in life. There are people in their 30s and 40s and 50s and they've got so much vitality and strength and productivity."

Of all the challenges facing the integrity of today's athletes, Davis believes the most difficult are those associated with sexual and emotional purity. In 18 years of experience around the University of Texas campus, he has seen firsthand the long-reaching effects that reckless lifestyles can have on its willing participants.

"This is how I describe it to the hundreds of kids I get to teach every other week: The quality of your relationships ultimately affects the quality of your sports performance," Davis says. "This is the formula: Healthy relationships produce low stress, or a happy heart, which produces peak performance. So healthy relationships, where you're serving and respecting others and you're pursuing purity, create low stress, and that produces peak performance. The opposite is true too. Bad relationships create high stress, which produces low performance."

Yet there's an even greater danger that comes with a life that rejects the concept of physical and emotional purity. Davis says it's a consequence that penetrates the skin, migrates beyond the muscles and bypasses the bones.

"Spiritually, it cuts you off from fellowship with God," Davis warns. "It tarnishes your testimony. It puts you in a tough position to minister to other people and to be an ambassador for Christ. Emotionally, it causes a lot of stress."

Davis knows a little something about being an ambassador for Christ. As a member of the 1996 and 2000 U.S. Olympic teams, he had the unique opportunity to not only represent his country but also to share his faith with the masses from a lofty platform. As a member of three swimming relay teams, Davis earned three gold medals in the 1996 Games (the most of any male competitor) and two silver medals in the 2000 Games.

The success brought with it endorsements, television appearances and the opportunity to embark on a career as both a motivational speaker and a master clinician. But for Davis, it's the chance to speak into the lives of young people that most intrigues him. It's his hope that he can share with them the message of integrity through Christ that has long-term ramifications for this life and the life to come.

"When you help people look at life from that long-term perspective of where they want to be when they're 70 or 80 or what they want people to read about in their obituary, you realize just how important it is to pursue integrity above everything else," Davis concludes. "Making the hard decisions early in life will make your life easier later."

TRAINING TIME

1. Josh Davis says that as a hotshot swimmer at the University of Texas, "My identity and my value came from my sport instead of God." What are some of the things for which you are known? Have you ever found yourself—like Davis—wrapped up in those things?

2. It took a serious illness at the end of Davis's freshman year to get his attention. Can you describe a time when God went to extreme measures to send a message to you? How did that bottom-of-the-barrel experience inspire you to rethink your concept of integrity?

3. Read Ephesians 4:25-32; 5:3-5,18. What are some of the things Paul tells us will separate us from God's kingdom? What are some other dangers that might accompany these things? What are some of the ways you can keep them out of your life?

4. Read 1 Corinthians 6:19-20. What do you think Paul means when he says that "you were bought at a price"? How might understanding that fact change the way you approach your physical relationships? Your lifestyle choices? Your health? Your reputation?

5. Read John 10:10. Where can you find true life and true freedom? Has John 10:10 proven to be true in your life? If so, how?

"In 2001, I had taken most of the year off after the 2000 Olympics. But because I eat well and sleep well, I showed up to nationals and qualified for the finals to go to the world championships with basically no training. All of my teammates were kind of ticked off that I got to do that. They take eight guys for the finals, and my buddy on the team got ninth. I decided to scratch and let him have the eighth spot, because even though I earned a spot on the travel team, I knew in good conscience I wasn't training full-time, and I didn't want to be on the U.S.A. team without a full effort. I also had other things to consider. My wife was pregnant, and I didn't want to be away from home. So I scratched and gave him the spot, and he swam that night and made the team. He told me, 'Man, I owe you a steak dinner,' because that basically got him his salary for the next year. Now, my friend wasn't one of the guys who drank and partied the most, but the moral of the story is that you can have guys who train their brains out but don't know how to make healthy decisions outside of the pool, because they are enslaved to drinking and dysfunctional relationships. I will take my good Christian living and no training over their hard training and messed-up living anytime."

—Josh Davis

Boldly Go

Jon Kitna
NFL Quarterback

And who will harm you if you are passionate for what is good?
But even if you should suffer for righteousness, you are blessed.
Do not fear what they fear or be disturbed, but set apart the Messiah
as Lord in your hearts, and always be ready to give a defense to
anyone who asks you for a reason for the hope that is in you.

1 PETER 3:13-15

Be bold, be bold, and everywhere be bold.

HERBERT SPENCER

To achieve any kind of success in life takes a certain measure of courage and boldness. This is especially true for the athlete who must believe in his or her talents and abilities enough to chase after a lofty set of goals.

Jon Kitna is certainly no exception to that rule. As the Detroit Lions' starting quarterback, he has come a long way, thanks mostly to an uncanny confidence in his ability—even when most others failed to recognize what the scrappy athlete had to offer. It's that same confidence—a confidence that he developed growing up on the unsavory east side of Tacoma, Washington—that Kitna believes has allowed him the opportunity to be a unifying force in every locker room he's ever occupied.

"I think it goes back to my upbringing," Kitna says. "I was brought up in a very diverse situation and went to a Boys and Girls Club in first grade, so I can relate to a lot of different types of people. So maybe that's one thing. I don't only feel comfortable in one kind of setting; I feel comfortable in a lot of different settings. And in a locker room, there are a lot of different settings in there."

At Lincoln High School in Tacoma, Kitna was a star athlete in football, basketball and baseball. He was driven to excel in all of his competitive pursuits, and that drive pushed him far enough to gain a spot playing for Central Washington University. As a freshman in 1992, he was so far down the depth chart that he had to beg the receivers coach for a football he could toss around during practices. Kitna's determination eventually paid off, and by his sophomore season, he was the starting signal caller.

Life as the proverbial Big Man on Campus came with its perks, and Kitna openly admits that early on in his career at Central Washington, he took full advantage of everything afforded to him. According to an article by David Fleming, written for ESPN.com, Kitna spent most of the 1993 season drinking, swearing, fighting, shoplifting and sleeping around on his girlfriend, Jennifer. After she found him in bed with another woman, he made the decision to get back into church and allow God to straighten him out once and for all. He and Jennifer were married 10 months later, and the couple has never looked back.

Another huge part of Kitna's spiritual growth came through the ministry of Fellowship of Christian Athletes. He says that the man who led him to Christ was an active speaker around town. Kitna would go where the man was speaking whenever he could, just to listen because he was "enthralled" with God's Word. Now, almost 15 years later, Kitna sees an even greater need for ministries such as FCA to help train young athletes about godly integrity.

"We're seeing an epidemic at the professional level of people who have been successful in athletics but have no idea how to be successful in life," Kitna says. "We've got it backward. We say that if the pros weren't doing what they were doing, the kids in high school wouldn't be doing what they are doing. But that's wrong, because once they get to the pros, it's hard for them to change patterns, behaviors and habits. But if coaches can take these kids at the high-school level and teach the character of that person instead of just who he is as a player, then what's going to happen is he'll go to college and he'll gain more character. Then when he gets to the pros and gets success and money and has all this power and these things, he's got the character to go along with it. Then he'll be a good model for those kids back in high school."

Kitna doesn't just support the concept of reaching out to young people with his words. He follows through with his actions. Kitna started a ministry at Remann Hall in Tacoma and regularly recruits teammates to join him in hanging out with troubled teens. He donates tickets to Lions' home games to the Boys and Girls Club and meets with the kids afterwards. It's for the express purpose of teaching true character—Christ-centered integrity—that Kitna faithfully creates his own ministry opportunities and backs up those within the ministry of FCA.

"[What FCA is] doing in the high school and college levels is really where it's at," Kitna says. "Because that's where you're gonna get kids to change. And I just encourage things that they're teaching. Be bold. Be strong. And teach these kids boundaries. Teach them what the Bible says. If we know what the Bible says, then we have to make a choice, and if the Spirit's in you, you'll make the right choice."

By Kitna's senior season at Central Washington University in 1995, he had led the Wildcats to the NAIA National Football Championship. He finished his career with 99 touchdowns, completing 58 percent of his passes for 12,353 yards. Despite the stellar performance, Kitna was not invited to the 1996 NFL Combine; however, teammate Jamie Christian (and cousin to Dennis Erickson, Seattle's coach at the time) helped him set up a workout day with the Seahawks. Erickson was impressed with Kitna's accuracy and signed him as a free agent.

Kitna ended up playing for the Barcelona Dragons of the now-defunct NFL Europe. He finished the season as the MVP runner-up and claimed the World Bowl MVP title after throwing for 401 yards and two touchdowns against the Rhein Fire in 1997. Two years later, he had fought his way to the starting spot in Seattle before leaving as an unrestricted free agent and signing with Cincinnati, where he earned the 2003 NFL Comeback Player of the Year award but ultimately lost his starting job to number-one draft pick Carson Palmer.

Kitna joined the Detroit Lions as an unrestricted free agent in 2006 and not only earned the starting spot but was also named team captain. In his first season, he set team records for completions and attempts and became just the second passer in Detroit history to throw for 4,000 yards. More importantly, his teammates began to embrace him as a spiritual leader as well.

"People are very perceptive, so you have to be yourself," Kitna says. "You can't be somebody you're not. I've seen guys try to fake being a leader. I've seen guys try to be rah-rah guys who weren't. I've seen guys try to be tough guys and all that, but that's not who they were. People see right through that and say, 'I'm not going to follow that.' They know that when times get tough, you won't be who you are right now. They're not going to follow that."

This unlikely hero also recognizes that in addition to his on-the-field leadership skills, his courage to share Christ with others has likewise increased over the duration of his career. Kitna says that it all boils down to living with integrity, which comes from the ultimate source.

"I think you become bolder the more you read the Bible," Kitna says. "And my pastor says this back home all the time. He says that most people don't believe the Bible because they don't know what it says. Most people don't read the Bible. Most people don't understand what the Bible really says. They don't really understand who Jesus was."

One example that Kitna sites is found in Romans 12, which talks about God's mercy and the sacrifice that Jesus made on the cross, which in turn requires believers to become "a living sacrifice, holy and pleasing to God" as an act of "spiritual worship" (v. 1).

"What do I have to be afraid of?" Kitna asks. "I've been saved from an eternity in hell. It's mind-boggling to me because sometimes I am timid, or I am intimidated by certain situations. I think, *You know, maybe I shouldn't say anything. I don't want to rub anybody the wrong way.* That's ridiculous. What I have to put up with in the locker room or in certain situations on the field—if I have to put up with some of the things that *they* say or some of their opinions, some of what they have to say, you know what? They can hear what I have to say too."

Despite Kitna's solid year in 2006, the team still struggled and finished 3-13. But behind the scenes, things were changing dramatically. Team unity was improving, and several players made commitments to Christ. That led to an even more vocal stance among the Christian players. It wasn't always popular with their unsaved teammates, but

Kitna says that didn't stop him and his fellow believers from speaking boldly and honestly.

"I think that we should speak the truth," Kitna says. "In the locker room, we try to speak the truth. We don't go around pointing out things to everybody, but if they want to ask a question, what they're saying is, 'I want to know the truth. I want to know what the Bible says.' And ultimately, that's what every person really wants to know. What *is* the truth? And as I look at Jesus' life, He was one that always saw the good in somebody *around* the bad. And I always remind myself, *What have I been forgiven of? Where would I be if it were not for Christ?* And when I do that, it's a little easier for me to be in the locker room and handle situations that come up."

Heading into 2007, the Lions had high hopes for a big turnaround. Kitna was so confident, in fact, that he predicted during preseason press interviews that his team would win 10 games. Early on, Kitna looked as if he might be a prophet, as the team started out 6-2. But a disappointing follow-up (including 6 consecutive losses) resulted in a 7-9 season.

Kitna then found himself under fire for a wide array of circumstances. The team's failure to secure a winning record—much less make it to 10 victories—allowed naysayers the opportunity to take swipes at Kitna's outspoken Christian beliefs. He also suffered through an embarrassing bit of bad publicity when he attended a team Halloween party dressed semi-naked in a costume along with his wife who was dressed as a fast-food drive-thru attendant. The couple was poking fun at defensive line coach Joe Cullen, who in August 2006 had driven naked through a drive-thru window at a fast-food restaurant. Kitna admitted in hindsight that he had made a poor decision.

In that situation, Kitna was reminded of how precarious one's integrity can truly be. He also knows that there are pitfalls lurking around every corner that force him to stay on guard and to keep his emotions and attitude in check. "I know what God has told me," Kitna says. "I've seen God working in my past. But you can have a bad practice or there might be something a coach says to you, and the enemy will just use that and start throwing those flaming arrows—just throwing those accusations at you, trying to get you to doubt your destiny, to doubt that God has a plan for your life. And in this game, it can change every day.

"Early on in my career, I didn't recognize spiritual warfare," he adds. "I didn't really know about it. It took a pastor back home when I was playing with the Seahawks to teach me about spiritual battles. There're times when you'll go to the line of scrimmage and the enemy's telling you that 'You're gonna throw an interception here.' All the time that happens to me. 'You're gonna fumble this snap.' Those are battles that you're fighting all the time. . . . If I'm a child of God, that's not natural for me to think that way. That can only come from the enemy."

One of Kitna's biggest weapons in this spiritual battle is the Word of God. In particular, he uses the victory prayer found in Psalm 35: "Oppose my opponents, LORD; fight those who fight me. Take Your shields—large and small—and come to my aid" (vv. 1-2). David later writes in verse 9, "Then I will rejoice in the LORD; I will delight in His deliverance."

"[Satan's] attacking all the time," Kitna says. "He's trying to tempt you into doing things that might destroy your marriage. In this business, there's lots of ways that you could stray. And last year, he attacked this team. All these guys were getting saved, and their marriages were getting better. They were coming to know the Lord, and [Satan was] attacking their marriages, trying to divide their marriages. And I remember a time last year walking out of the building, just screaming to myself, 'Devil, bring it on, because my God is bigger than you! And Jesus Christ is bigger than you!' And I've been taught how to pray offensive prayer and just praying in the name of Jesus, that He comes against the spiritual warfare."

But ultimately, Kitna's ability to be bold with his faith is only as strong as his foundation of integrity and character. It's the same way for all of us. With integrity comes respect, and with respect comes people's attention. Others may not always agree, but they will at least give men and women of great character the chance to be heard.

As it says in 1 Peter 3:13-15 (one of Kitna's favorite Scriptures), "Do not fear what they fear or be disturbed, but set apart the Messiah as Lord in your hearts, and always be ready to give a defense to anyone who asks you for a reason for the hope that is in you."

"The most important thing is to live my life with Christ set apart as Lord of my life," Kitna says. "If I set apart Christ as Lord of my life, I don't have to go and beat people over the head with it; they'll come to me and ask questions. Because that's what the rest of the verse says: Be prepared to give an *answer* for the hope that you have when people ask you questions. Do it with gentleness and respect. . . . But at the same time, it doesn't give me an excuse not to be bold and preach not what Christ has done for me, but what the cross means to *everyone*."

If there's one thing Kitna understands about the character of Christ, it's the fact that He was bold. When Kitna reads chapters two and three from the book of Revelation, he sees a bold representation of Jesus talking to the different churches—giving them commendation but also giving them a healthy dose of rebuke and instruction.

And as far as Kitna is concerned, it's that balance between discipline and grace—rooted in a solid foundation of truth—that he also hopes to achieve in his life as a father, a husband, a professional athlete and, most importantly, a follower of Jesus.

"A lot of people misconstrue who Christ really was," Kitna says. "They want to say He was just loving and just totally accepting of everyone. And yeah, He *did* love everyone, but He did not accept everything that everybody did. He told you the truth."

TRAINING TIME

1. Read 1 Thessalonians 5:12-23. What are some of the admonitions that might directly impact your leadership skills? What are some specific situations where adhering to one of these teachings might make the difference between success and failure?

2. Kitna talks about how the relational elements found in FCA helped him develop spiritually. What are some of the organizations with which you are involved? What are some of the benefits that accompany that kind of fellowship?

3. Kitna believes that "you become bolder the more you read the Bible." How can a strong knowledge of God's Word increase your boldness when sharing your faith with others? What happens to your boldness when you aren't as confident in your biblical knowledge?

4. Kitna says, "[God] allows some times of trial, some times of hardship to develop a testimony." What situation in your life helped you to develop your testimony? How did that allow you to glorify God?

5. Read 1 Peter 3:13-15. What does this Scripture tell you about fear? What are some ways that you can "be ready to give a defense to anyone who asks you for a reason for the hope that is in you"?

"It's interesting because when I first got saved, I was in college, and none of the guys in our locker room knew me then. So I can share my testimony with them and all that, but one thing that God has always done when He's taken me from a situation where people knew me and taken me to a new situation, He establishes a testimony in that situation. He allows me to go through some perceived hard times on the outside. And typically that's within the football realm. And you go through something where maybe the fans are booing you and you get benched, or you lose your job, or whatever it may be. And that develops a testimony amongst your teammates of, 'Okay, here's something that happened to this guy, and things aren't always just perfect, and how does he handle that? How does he handle it differently? How does he carry himself?' And that's one thing that God has always done in my career: Whenever I'm put in a new situation—and that was when I first came to the Seahawks, when I went to Cincinnati and now with Detroit—He allows some times of trial, some times of hardship to develop a testimony that people can look and say, 'Okay, this guy's the real deal.' So I just try to be myself and to be honest. And whatever it is, it seems to be something that people are somewhat attracted to in some way."

—Jon Kitna

8

THE ROAD LESS TRAVELED

Lorenzo Romar
Head NCAA Men's Basketball Coach

Enter through the narrow gate. For the gate is wide and the road is broad that leads to destruction, and there are many who go through it. How narrow is the gate and difficult the road that leads to life, and few find it.

MATTHEW 7:13-14

The ultimate measure of a man is not where he stands in moments of comfort and convenience, but where he stands at times of challenge and controversy.

MARTIN LUTHER KING, JR.

For Lorenzo Romar, integrity is one of the simplest concepts he's ever learned—so simple, it only takes a brief, pondering pause followed by a concisely spoken sentence for him to explain.

"A person with integrity consistently does the right thing," he matter-of-factly states.

As the University of Washington men's basketball coach, Romar has provided a walking, talking example of integrity to the young athletes that don the Huskies' uniform year in and year out.

Take for example the coach's no-swearing policy. During practices and games, players are not allowed to use any form of profanity. If they do, the penalty is a healthy number of laps around the court. Romar says it's not even necessarily a spiritual matter but rather an issue of self-control and class.

"What I found is that guys will not use cuss words around me off the court, but I never told them that," Romar says. "Off the court I've told them, 'That's your life. But on the court when people are watching how we conduct ourselves, that's disrespectful to some and offends some. So stay away from it.'"

Romar's strong disciplinarian style is in sharp contrast to much of what he experienced growing up in Compton—the rough-and-tumble Los Angeles community popularized within hip-hop culture. All around him were signs of family breakdown, but Romar—who says he wouldn't want to have grown up anywhere else—is thankful for his parents, who raised him in a household built on integrity.

"There was crime and some other things that weren't good, but I did my best to stay away from those things," Romar says. "I couldn't come home if I did something I had no business doing. I also had a desire to be something special in this sport, and I knew that the other peripheral things could get me off track, so there was no interest in them at all."

Romar fell in love with basketball around the age of 10. His passion for the sport was strong enough to drive a self-described average talent all the way from street ball to the NBA. But along the way, the wild playground player needed some taming. That, Romar says, happened at Cerritos Community College and then the University of Washington, where he had a chance to play for the legendary Marv Harshman.

"My junior-college coaches began the process," Romar says. "It was the first time I had really been coached in my life. Then Marv Harshman was able to help me see the more fundamentally sound parts of the game. When I did decide I wanted to get into coaching, one of the things I thought about was how much of an impact a coach could have on his players."

Romar's college coaches also provided a template for integrity that would stick with him for years to come. And while the young athlete had not yet committed his life to Christ, he knew by the examples of his parents and coaches that there was something more to living right than just abiding by the laws of the land.

"If I'm a male and I'm 22 years old and I'm in and out of different ladies' beds, partying from time to time, then as far as the world would be concerned, they would say you're just being a man," Romar says. "Now if I were to rob or steal, then I would have crossed the line. But God's standard is different. God wants us to be pure until marriage. That's just one example. To hold a grudge or to seek revenge, the world would say, 'Yep, I can't blame him for that. They shouldn't have crossed him.' But God says, 'Vengeance is mine' and Jesus talked about forgiveness. So there are two different standards, and you can have a worldly standard and still be looked upon as a man of integrity. I think there is a difference, and I probably fit that mold before I became a Christian. I knew what I was doing behind closed doors, but others didn't. And if they did know, they'd say, 'Well, there's nothing wrong with that. Everybody does that.' "

While Romar admits that he struggled with Christ-centered integrity off the court, his relentless work ethic paved the way for significant success on the court. As a senior, he was named team captain; and during both his years at Washington, he was the recipient of the team's Most Inspirational Award.

Romar's unique combination of desire, discipline and sheer determination ultimately afforded him the opportunity to play in the NBA, where in 1980 he was drafted in the seventh round by Golden State. He spent his first three seasons with the Warriors and another season split between the Milwaukee Bucks and the Detroit Pistons. During that time, he was surrounded by greatness, including head coach Don Nelson and such perennial All-Stars as Bernard King and Sidney Moncrief. It was a surreal existence that left him feeling like a kid in a candy store.

But the giddiness that occasionally overcame Romar as a rookie quickly wore off, and he suddenly began to realize that something was missing in his life. There was a void in his heart that the NBA experience could never truly fill.

"I had always believed in God and wanted to have a relationship with God, but I just didn't know how to do it," Romar says. "I was raised in a church where the only time they would open the Bible was when the minister would open it himself and read from some already-picked-out Scriptures. He'd talk for 10 minutes about the gospel, and that was it. And that was fine at the time; but there came a point where I just felt like, *What would happen if I died? There's got to be more.*"

Romar's quest was spurred by a friend who challenged him to start reading the Bible and exploring its truths for himself. He was encouraged to make up his own mind and stop relying on what he had heard others preach and teach. On September 10, 1983, Romar and his wife, Leona, both accepted Christ, thanks in part to the personal revelations that awaited him at the end of the soul-searching process.

"I realized that I was trying to be right with God by doing good works, by being a good person," Romar says. "I read [in the Bible] that [doing good works] didn't matter. That didn't make you have a relationship with the Lord, because we couldn't be good enough. We'll always fall short."

While Romar's new life in Christ was just beginning, his NBA career was less than two years from coming to a close. That's not to say his playing days were over. In fact, while trying out for the Indiana Pacers prior to the 1985-86 season, he was contacted by Athletes in Action, the athletic division of Campus Crusade for Christ. At the time, AIA had a long-standing basketball tradition in which former college players would travel during the collegiate preseason to play exhibitions against major universities all across the country. Romar was attracted to AIA while still in high school and sent them a tape in the hope of playing for them one day.

"I'd love to say I turned the NBA down to play with AIA, but I didn't," Romar admits. "I was in a situation where I didn't know if I was going to make a team. I had a tryout, but I didn't know if I was going to make it. I had just become a Christian; and this was an opportunity to tell thousands about my faith in Jesus Christ and still be involved in the game, so I went for it."

Romar spent seven seasons with AIA and started in 224 of 233 games. In 1992 (and at the age of 34), he scored 45 points against Michigan's famous Fab Five freshmen—a group that featured Chris Webber, Juwan Howard and Jalen Rose—and went on to play in the NCAA championship game later that year. Romar concluded his playing career as AIA's record holder in single-game points (54), single-game assists (21) and all-time assists (1,689). Romar also ranks second among AIA's scorers (4,244 points).

During that time, Romar says he enjoyed dispelling the myth that Christian athletes were soft and not as talented by routinely competing with, and often defeating, teams that were considered heavy favorites. But more importantly, he was able to minister to basketball fans in the United States and abroad, as well as to hundreds of incarcerated criminals.

AIA also afforded Romar his first opportunity to lead his own team—first as a player-coach and then as the head coach. Thanks to the prodding of Mark Gottfried—a fellow AIA alum and current head coach at Alabama—Romar eventually landed on Jim Harrick's staff at UCLA. Four years later, Romar earned his first head coaching job at Pepperdine, where he led the Waves to a National Invitational Tournament bid in his third and final season. Following the turnaround of that program, he took the head coaching position at St. Louis, where the Billikens claimed the Conference USA tournament title and an NCAA bid in his first of three seasons.

But when Romar was courted by Washington to replace Bob Bender in March 2002, the former Husky had an instant gut feeling that told him he was meant to coach his alma mater all along. After struggling to a 10-17 record in that first season, Romar led his team to four consecutive NCAA tournament berths and three straight appearances in the Sweet 16.

Before Romar could enjoy the fruits of his labor, he first was forced to overcome a challenge to his personal integrity. Cameron Dollar, one of Romar's assistants and a former star player at UCLA, was cited for 28 recruiting violations involving the contact of prospective athletes during periods of time in which such contact is not allowed by NCAA rules. As the head coach, Romar was held responsible for the breech of ethical conduct.

"It was something that was very difficult for me, because I had always envisioned having a program that was spotless and without reproach, and that kind of cut into that," Romar says. "That was tough, but we got beyond it, and I thought we handled it the right way. But at the same time, that is something I want people to be able to say—not so they can say, 'Lorenzo Romar is a man of integrity,' but ultimately so they can see why we do it the right way. It's because I have a relationship with Jesus Christ. That is my guiding force and motivating force."

105

Since then, Romar has reclaimed that squeaky-clean image and has managed to win without even the slightest bending of the rules. That doesn't mean the temptation to do so isn't lurking around the corner of every high-school campus on which he steps foot.

"There are times when you are not allowed to have face-to-face contact with kids, and there are some coaches who will say, 'No, we'll set it up, and we'll meet you somewhere,'" Romar explains. "And they'll say, 'Nobody will know.' And I say, 'But I'll know.' So I've been able to avoid that. And then sometimes other college coaches who are recruiting the same kid will take advantage of those situations. Sometimes the kids will think, *Washington must not be as interested. They didn't meet with me.* And you have to try to explain why you didn't. That's where you say, 'God will honor it.'"

Since taking the high-profile Pac-10 Conference job at the University of Washington, Romar has especially felt the heat from those within the media and some within the ranks of higher education who disapprove of his active involvement in ministry-related activities. He has been the subject of national news stories discussing the appropriateness of coaches at state-funded universities incorporating their beliefs in the job setting.

And while Romar contends that he has never "crossed the line," he always does his best to balance the display of his open-ended faith with a very public life. Much of that ability to successfully juggle the two came from his seven years with AIA, where he regularly spoke at public schools and learned what he could and couldn't say about God.

"Everything that I'm able to do, I do," Romar says. "No one can put me in jail because I tell them what changed my life. No one can keep me from telling my personal testimony. I can do that anytime I want. This is not a daily thing where I'm trailing everybody on the team with a Bible in my hand. Sometimes I try to explain why certain decisions are made, and we provide opportunities for kids to go to Bible studies. We just try to create an environment that would make someone say, 'It's a little different here than other places I've been, and I like it.'"

One of Romar's favorite Scriptures is Ephesians 5:1, which admonishes believers to "be imitators of God." "If I can keep that perspective, I am basically living out a script as if I were an actor," Romar says. "I'm not talking about being phony, but I've taken on a different attitude, a different outlook. I see everything through that outlook as I'm guided by my coach or my producer—which is Christ—as opposed to my own views, my fleshly worldly views."

Romar says that when the temptation to cave in to his own humanity is strong, he immediately reminds himself of the damage such a moral failure would do to his witness and any future opportunities he might have to share the gospel. He also relies heavily on the prompting of the Holy Spirit, which helps keep him accountable to the Christ-centered life of integrity.

"There have been times when I've made mistakes," Romar admits. "I'm not perfect. But I'm aware of those mistakes, and I'm miserable when I have made mistakes. That's a big, big difference between a man with integrity and a Christian with integrity. I think you can be a man of integrity without being a Christian and not feel guilty when you do it your way. If you've got the Spirit of God living in you, man, you're going to be miserable if you don't do it His way.

"The best way to go through life is to be a man of integrity," Romar concludes. "Living a life of integrity does not mean you're missing out on anything. You're not. You're actually going to discover the fun part of life. Integrity is ultimately being a man of God."

107

TRAINING TIME

1. Romar talks about "two different standards" of integrity. Can you give some specific differences between worldly integrity and godly integrity? What are some problems that might arise from living by the world's standard of integrity?

2. Read Ephesians 5:1. In what ways does imitating God change your attitude and your outlook? How might it affect the choices that you make and, ultimately, your integrity?

3. Can you describe a time when your public expressions of faith sparked a negative response? How did that make you feel? Read Luke 12:11-12. What does this Scripture say is the best way to handle situations such as those?

4. Romar says, "Living a life of integrity doesn't mean you're missing out on anything." Why do you think so many people believe that living according to the Bible is boring and unadventurous?

5. Romar tells how he maintained integrity while recruiting prospective athletes. How can doing something simple such as following the rules allow you to share your faith with others? Can you describe a similar circumstance in your life when your actions spoke louder than words?

"There's a particular coach at a high school where we were recruiting a young man who is in the NBA now. There are certain days when you can't have face-to-face contact with kids. One day, we were in the coach's office, and the kid that we were recruiting came by with a couple other players, and they just sat down in the office with the coach. I remember saying to the coach, 'Well, you know what? I really can't talk to him, so I'm probably going to have to step outside.' And he said, 'No, no, no, no, no. They can leave.' And they left. I was at St. Louis at the time, and I just got this note from him. It says, 'I have rooted for the Huskies ever since you arrived. Ever since we met, I have looked up to you as a coach of character and a positive influence for the rest of the coaches.' To my knowledge, this coach was not a Christian. I never talked to him about the Lord or my character. He just saw that I was going to do things the right way. . . . The Bible says they'll know we are Christians if we love one another. That is perhaps the best way to show that Christ is making a difference in your life. I can sit here and tell you that I'm going to get called up into heaven, I'm so holy. But it won't matter if my actions don't back that up."

—Lorenzo Romar

9

Trial by Fire

Laura Wilkinson
U.S. Gold Medalist in Diving

And not only that, but we also rejoice in our afflictions, because we know that affliction produces endurance, endurance produces proven character, and proven character produces hope.

Romans 5:3-4

My strength is the strength of ten, because my heart is pure.

Alfred Lord Tennyson

When Laura Wilkinson says she used to be a very quiet and shy person, it's a little hard to believe. That's because these days, the outgoing, personable world-class diver is one of sports' most outspoken Christian athletes.

Wilkinson is also very articulate when it comes to matters of faith. She strives to live with integrity in an effort to maintain solid footing on the broad platform that worldwide notoriety as an Olympic gold medalist has afforded her.

"I've had to learn to speak up for God in my life," Wilkinson says. "I've realized that if He has a presence in my heart, He needs to have a presence in everything. If

He's really the center of my life, He's really going to be involved in everything."

The foundation for Wilkinson's faith was poured early in her life. Growing up in the Houston suburb of Spring, Texas (she now resides in The Woodlands), she cites her parents, Ed and Linda Wilkinson, as her first examples of integrity and as the driving force behind her initial interest in a relationship with God.

"I became a Christian at a very young age," Wilkinson says. "I was eight years old, and it just made sense. I was like, *Why wouldn't people do this?* I totally got it, and I was really excited about God. Then I entered my freshman year of high school, and I switched churches. I started going to a youth group with one of my friends, and I started to see that some of the kids would be one way at church, and then we'd go to McDonald's or something like that after church, and they would be totally different. I just felt really uncomfortable, and I didn't know how to handle it. So I just stopped going, which is the complete opposite of what I should have done. At that point, I got confused, so I walked away from it, but then I ended up becoming just like them."

At the end of her freshman year in high school, when she was 15, Wilkinson discovered diving. She had actually started her competitive career as a seven-year-old gymnast, but a growth spurt made her realize that she "wasn't going to be the next Mary Lou Retton." Her gymnastics background did, however, help speed up her transition to the pool, and within two years she was competing on the

111

U.S. national team. That same year, Wilkinson won a bronze medal at the 1995 World Cup in the platform synchro event with partner Patty Armstrong.

By the time she graduated from high school and arrived at the University of Texas at Austin, where she had been offered an athletic scholarship for her diving skills, she was already a rising star within the American diving community. Wilkinson solidified that by winning NCAA titles in 1997 and 1999 and eight All-American honors. Along the way, she continued a streak of appearances on the national team that has stretched for 13 consecutive years and counting.

But while Wilkinson was emerging as the sport's next big thing, her spiritual life was sinking deeper every day. She knew she wasn't living for God anymore and was—with painful futility—trying desperately to call her own shots. Then, like the sting that comes from a badly missed dive, she was jarred back to her senses.

"My sophomore year in college, I realized that me being in control of my life just made a mess of things," Wilkinson says. "I knew that I needed God back. I didn't hit rock bottom, but it felt like it. So I totally recommitted my life, and it's just been different ever since."

Thanks to the example set by her parents, Wilkinson already had a working knowledge of what biblical, Christ-centered integrity looked like. She knew that some of the biggest keys to keeping integrity intact were attitude, perspective and focus. As Wilkinson grew stronger in her faith as a young adult, she also understood that it also required some sacrifices.

"There are definitely friends who I don't see as much anymore that I would like to," she says. "We don't really believe in the same stuff, so we don't really hang out as much anymore. That's kind of hard sometimes, but as much as you try to be an example to them, sometimes that really turns them off, or it affects you because you'll want to go out and do things that you shouldn't be doing. It's affected some friendships, which is tough. But I've also made new ones, which is wonderful."

For Wilkinson, the benefit of living a life with integrity is first and foremost the fact that it pleases God with the offering of obedience. She has also received an immeasurable, spiritual peace. And any emotional holes that may have been left after the loss of a friend or two have been replaced by her rewarding marriage to Eriek Hulseman.

Of course, Wilkinson has likewise been blessed with athletic success that arguably makes her the most decorated female diver in U.S. history. Her collective accomplishments include more than 30 major national and international gold medals. Wilkinson is also the first woman of any nationality to win platform gold medals at the World Championship (2005), the World Cup (2004) and the Olympics (2000), not to mention her gold-medal performance at the 1998 Goodwill Games.

With that kind of hardware, it would be easy to let one's guard down when it comes to maintaining a high level of integrity. But not for Wilkinson, who says her place in the spotlight makes it even that much more important that she abide by the same standards in public and in private. And that requires a healthy dose of internal honesty.

"I think being honest with yourself is like being the same you everywhere you go," Wilkinson says. "You can hide from yourself too. It's easy to tell yourself how great you are and blame all of your problems on someone else. But when you can take responsibility for your bad decisions, it will help you make the right decision the next time. You do need to be honest with yourself, and it's not easy all the time. It's just our human nature to pat ourselves on the back and think we're great, but it's not about us. We need to be making the decisions that God wants us to make."

Wilkinson's discussion of honesty and integrity reminds her of the fictional story that has become a staple of mass emails across the Internet. The tale describes a police officer who pulls over a woman for reckless driving. He notices several bumper stickers on the car that lead him to believe the car belongs to a person of faith. When the officer arrives at the window, he says to the woman, "This car obviously belongs to a Christian, so it must be stolen. Please step out of the vehicle."

It's a sad illustration of how many believers give the rest of the world a bad impression of what it means to follow Jesus. Wilkinson tries diligently to avoid becoming more than a punch line in the way that she lives her own life.

"If I'm advertising or if I'm saying that I'm a Christian and I represent Christ, I need to really represent Him in everything," she says. "I think that goes along with living it out in every aspect of your life—not being a different person to appease people at school or at work. You need to be the same person representing the same God everywhere you go."

But Wilkinson's most educational lessons on the subject of integrity have come from firsthand experiences that have tried her physically, emotionally and spiritually. During her career, she has suffered broken bones on three occasions and has dealt with three surgeries (only one of which was related to a broken bone).

It was an injury that took place just months before the 2000 U.S. Olympic trials that nearly pushed Wilkinson over the edge. She broke three metatarsals in her right foot, and the decision she made to leave school that year in order to pursue Olympic glory seemed like the wrong choice. Even prior to the injury, Wilkinson says her dream was getting fuzzy; she was losing her focus. But it didn't take long for her to realize how much she enjoyed diving and how badly she wanted to compete in Sydney, Australia.

"Breaking my foot was such a blessing in disguise," Wilkinson says. "When I first broke it, I was doing a thing with NBC where I was calling in and I would leave these messages. It was kind of like a voice-mail diary, and they were posting it. My husband saved them and put them all together in a song for me. I remember calling in the day after I broke my foot; and I said something like, 'This is really rough, and it hurts and it's tough, and I don't know what's going to happen, but I know that there's a silver lining in every dark cloud. When the clouds clear out, there will be rainbows.' I just knew that it wasn't the end."

For the next three months, Wilkinson fought through her challenging circumstance by using unconventional training methods. She would hop up the ladder to the 10-meter platform and sit on the edge in her street clothes. Wilkinson visualized her dives while exercising the accompanying arm motions. She also watched hours of video tape and concentrated on the mental side of diving.

Wilkinson adjusted her launch style by starting from a handstand position. This allowed her to avoid using that tender right foot while taking advantage of her gymnastics background. At the Olympic trials, she stunned the judges and the crowd by claiming a 40-point victory over the second-place competitor. Wilkinson then made a stunning comeback at the Olympics where she won the gold medal despite falling to fifth place after the first five dives.

Still unsure which victory was more special—the Olympics or the Olympic trials—Wilkinson does know one thing for sure: The perseverance she displayed throughout the entire process built her character in a way nothing else before ever had. Perhaps that's why one of her favorite Scriptures is Romans 5:3-4, in which the apostle Paul tells us that "we also rejoice in our afflictions, because we know that affliction produces endurance, endurance produces proven character, and proven character produces hope."

"I've had quite a few traumatic experiences in my life," Wilkinson says. "It helps knowing that God has made me to persevere and to keep going, even when things are difficult. I just need to trust Him. If I can't see beyond that big obstacle, God can see beyond it, and He's going to get me there. We might go right through the obstacle, or we might go around it, but I need to trust Him to get me there."

Wilkinson's story is much like the powerful passage of Scripture found in Malachi 3. In those prophetic verses, the writer foretells Jesus Christ's first appearance on Earth. In verse 2, Malachi compares the Savior to "a refiner's fire." In verse 3, he goes on to tell us how Jesus "will purify the sons of Levi and refine them like gold and silver."

Malachi uses the analogy of the purification process for fine metals to explain the sanctification, or refining, process that Christians must go through in order to become holy and acceptable before God. In Old Testament times, ore was placed in a crucible and heated at incredibly high temperatures. The heat caused the metal to separate from what was nonmetal, called "dross," which then floated to the top. This was drained off, leaving nearly pure metal.

For Wilkinson, it was the foot injury that ultimately took her through the same kind of purification and refining process that Malachi wrote about more than 2,000 years ago. "It's important to learn in those circumstances to thank God for the circumstances that maybe you don't appreciate," Wilkinson says. "For instance, when I broke my foot, I said to God, 'I know You have a plan for this, so I want to thank You for this and be joyful in this, even though it's painful and even though it's difficult. This is my fire. You're putting me through the fire, and You're going to mold me and make me into what I want to be.' To have the integrity to be able to thank Him in those moments is what I've been learning how to do."

When Wilkinson has a chance to speak to people—young and old alike—she always makes sure to tell them that a life of integrity isn't about a list of dos and don'ts that will take the fun out of life. Instead, she believes that rejecting the things of this world and accepting the things that come from heaven can result in "an awesome, adventurous life."

"Trusting God with my life and letting Him take me through storms has been more adventurous than any drug trip or any other worldly thing you can find," Wilkinson says. "When you actually can trust God fully and say yes to whatever He wants you to do and you follow Him, then that is an awesome adventure. That is more fulfilling than any worldly stuff you can get into. That other stuff isn't really living. It's like running away from life or avoiding things instead of really living."

There's no denying that Wilkinson has done some pretty spectacular things in her life thus far. Just by virtue of winning an Olympic gold medal, she has secured a place in history that can never be erased. But when it comes to spiritual matters such as integrity, Wilkinson is quick to point out just how ordinary and normal she is compared to the rest of us.

"I'm really no different from anyone else," she says. "I've screwed up big time in the past. I have to make a choice to get up every day and trust God and to have faith in Him and to choose His way and not just mine. That's what I want people to know. You don't just wake up one day and suddenly become this perfect person, and life is great and the sun is always shining. You're still a normal person. You've just chosen God's path, and you still have to choose that daily. It's not just choosing eternal life and then doing whatever you want. That's not how it is. You still have to make that choice every day.

"It's a choice that anyone can make," Wilkinson concludes. "You don't have to get cleaned up to go to God. He will take you just as you are. I think that's the biggest stumbling block that some people have. They know they might have to change, and that scares them. But go to God as you are, and He will clean you up and help you change, because you can't do that on your own."

TRAINING TIME

1. According to Laura Wilkinson, choosing to pursue biblical integrity sometimes means making sacrifices. What are some sacrifices you have made for the sake of integrity? What have been some of the benefits that have accompanied those sacrifices?

2. When it comes to integrity, how important is it for you to be honest with yourself? What are some of the dangers of not being honest with yourself? What are some ways you can avoid self-deception?

3. What are some of the areas of your life in which you are sometimes tempted to not represent Christ in all you do? How can these contradictions, if exposed, impact your ability to share the gospel with others?

4. Read Paul's words in Romans 5:3-4. In what ways does affliction produce endurance? How does endurance produce proven character? What is the relationship between proven character and hope? Can you relate a story in which these principles have manifested in your life?

5. Read Malachi 3:2-4. What are some things in your life that the refiner's fire might represent? How might troubling circumstances help purify your integrity? How can you be thankful and even joyful during hard times?

"Placing fifth at the 2004 Olympics was definitely disappointing, because I had won before; but I know well enough that fifth place in the Olympics is really good. I understand that. So I did appreciate it, because of what I did in my training, but at the same time my mission going in was to glorify God first and win a medal second. I didn't win a medal, but I did glorify God. I thanked Him in an interview. I don't think it ever aired, but that was the first thing out of my mouth. My whole attitude about it isn't what people expect. They always expect me to be all ticked off, but it was great. I loved Greece. It was a fantastic Olympics. Not medaling for me actually turned into fuel for a new passion that got lit for the sport again. I had to go through wrist surgery after that, and I thought maybe I'd just do one more year. I ended up winning the World Championships for the first time, and I started learning new dives. I mean, you don't start learning new dives when you're about to retire. I could just tell that I really wanted to keep doing this. Sometimes I'm not so sure, but then God will just put something back in my heart and remind me, 'This is what you're meant to do. This is what you love. I have you here because this is what I made you for.' "

—Laura Wilkinson

TAKING THE BATON

Duke Preston
NFL Offensive Lineman

*To Timothy, my dear son: Grace, mercy and peace from God the
Father and Christ Jesus our Lord. I have been reminded of your sincere
faith, which first lived in your grandmother Lois and in your mother
Eunice and, I am persuaded, now lives in you also. For this reason I
remind you to fan into flame the gift of God, which is in you through
the laying on of my hands. For God did not give us a spirit of timidity,
but a spirit of power, of love and of self-discipline.*

2 TIMOTHY 1:2,5-7, *NIV*

No legacy is so rich as honesty.
WILLIAM SHAKESPEARE

Duke Preston can still hear it now.

"Duke!"

His father's deep, booming voice echoed throughout
the cavernous racquetball court. Just moments earlier, assistant coach Raymond Preston had addressed his son's
freshman football team about a party that had taken place

the weekend before. The unsupervised event resulted in a substantial amount of underage drinking—including participation by the younger Preston.

And with his father's firm, beckoning call, Preston knew he was busted. "I turned around and walked back, and he said, 'I know you were at that party, and I know what went on at that party. Were you drinking?' And I said, 'Yeah, I guess I had a couple of sips.'"

As far as the young Preston was concerned, life as he knew it was about to end. But the next few words out of his father's mouth took him completely by surprise.

"I expected him to send me to the car, take me home and ground me for the week," Preston says. "But he just looked at me and he said, 'You say you want to be famous. You say you want to be a pro football player. You say you want to get a scholarship. You say you're a Christian. You say that you want to live your life for the Lord. But these things don't match up with that. If you really want to play pro football and live your life in a righteous way, those things aren't going to help you get there. In fact, they'll take you further away from your goals.'"

Still expecting the worst, Preston was even more astonished at his father's unexpected display of mercy and grace. "That's pretty much all he said, and I said, 'I know,'" Preston continues. "And then he said, 'It's up to you.' And that was all. I was like, *Wow!* He didn't yell at me. He didn't ground me. It was really cool to be enlightened like that in the way he chose to do it. It was a

123

great lesson at a young age in how to handle myself on and off the field and learning how my actions should match up with the words that I say and what I profess to be about."

To this day, that one moment in time remains a turning point in Preston's life. Even though it was one of the most defining moments he experienced with his father, it was in reality just part of a series of example-setting events that Preston had witnessed throughout his entire childhood and his early adulthood.

Now, as an offensive lineman for the Buffalo Bills, Preston carries that legacy of integrity with him everywhere he goes. It's a legacy that, from the beginning, he has equated with a greater understanding of Christ-centered values.

124

"Growing up in a Christian household like I did, my athletics and just my life were real God-centered from a young age," Preston says. "I correlated the integrity of my parents with biblical wisdom and biblical principles. Even before I was in high school, I always felt convicted. I could hear God speaking to me and really talking to my heart from a very young age in terms of knowing what He did and didn't want me to do. My parents' instructions were reinforcing the principles that I knew."

When Preston was three years old, his father retired from a successful NFL career with the San Diego Chargers. He never experienced that much of his father's life as a professional athlete, except for the occasional alumni games and special events. Preston believes that being around his dad minus the hype was beneficial to his future life in the pro ranks. It helped him understand the temporal nature of fame and fortune.

Preston and his sister were also blessed to constantly have their dad around, thanks to the sports-apparel business that their father ran out of their home. Not only was the elder Preston able to coach his son's baseball and football teams, but he was also afforded the opportunity to instill in his son the connective biblical values of integrity and excellence.

"Whatever you do, do it to the best of your ability," Preston says. "That was a key for me growing up. People ask me all the time if I felt pressure growing up with a dad who played nine years in the NFL. I really didn't simply because everything he stressed in our home was to do everything the right way and do it to the best of your ability. My dad always stressed that in everything.

"When he was coaching me in Little League baseball, he'd have us run a lap around the tree. We had to run all the way around the tree, not up to the tree or close enough to where you could almost touch it, but all the way around the tree. I'm positive that the reason why I'm where I'm at right now is because my dad taught me how to do things right and to do it right all of the time."

Another part of the legacy that Preston's father has passed along to him includes the heritage of his humble roots, which pushed him to great success as an athlete, an entrepreneur, a parent and, most importantly, a follower of Christ.

"Before my rookie year, I had about six weeks off, and I went and spent some time with my grandmother in the area where my dad grew up," Preston recalls. "I was able to see where he came from—which was just a poor neighborhood and a ghetto type of place—and then see him transcend that and move on beyond that. That made me think about the life I grew up with and how easily I could have been born in the same neighborhood where he lived. I have such an appreciation and respect for what he did to do that."

That visit not only made Preston appreciate his family's roots but also made him that much more grateful for the daily lessons of integrity, honesty and hard work that his father had passed along to him throughout his childhood and teenage years. That consistency inspired Preston to grab the proverbial baton from his father and carry it with him as he matured into adulthood.

"He had such a heart for instilling values in me and my sister," Preston says. "We did love God. God was in the center of everything we did. That's something that motivates me now—that I can be that example to a kid that I speak to and in the future whenever I might have children. It's definitely something that makes me proud to follow in my dad's footsteps, more so to be the Christian man that I am now as opposed to me playing in the NFL and following in his footsteps that way. The spiritual treasures that he's instilled in me are much more valuable to me than any type of football legacy that our family has."

After a successful football and basketball career at Mt. Carmel High School in San Diego, Preston went to play football for the University of Illinois, where he was a three-year starter at the center position. He quickly earned a reputation as an extremely intelligent athlete with an uncanny technical ability on the offensive line. In fact, over the course of his final two seasons, only one defender was able to break through his position to record a quarterback sack.

With a speech communication degree in hand, Preston entered the 2005 NFL Draft, where he was selected by the Buffalo Bills in the fourth round. In fact, he was the first center drafted out of Illinois in 13 years. But in his rookie season, he found himself mostly on the second string and seeing action off the bench as a center and an offensive guard (including one start for the injured Chris Villarrial) as well as a member of the special teams unit.

In 2006, Preston saw more time as a starter, again replacing Villarrial for much of the season's second half; and in 2007 he saw a good deal of playing time as the backup at three different positions (left guard, right guard and center). And even though Preston has yet to obtain superstar status, he still understands how the issue of pride and arrogance can creep into any pro athlete's life. He's even more acutely aware of the negative spiritual ramifications that accompany such a mindset.

"It's hard, because it's such a pseudo-reality," Preston says. "You're 23, 24, 25, 26 years old, and you're making a paycheck that's just absurd. Everyone wants to be your friend, and everyone wants to be around you. It's real easy to get caught up in what people think of you, and then all of the sudden you start to think more highly of yourself than you should. For me, it's just been a challenge to keep that same godly perspective and that same biblical perspective. God purposed me to be here. It's no accident that I'm in Buffalo. It's no accident that I was drafted where I was. I have to keep the perspective that God has something He wants me to do for His purpose here. It shouldn't be about me and all that I have. All of that stuff comes with it when you're living according to God's purpose."

Preston says he has felt a calling on his life from a very young age. It was that strong conviction to follow God that caused him to stay true to a life of prayer and Bible devotion. In times of trouble or moments of doubt, Preston would look to the Word for direction. Even in something as simple as being nervous over pitching a Little League baseball game for the first time, he turned to Romans 8:31 and reminded himself that "if God is for us, who is against us?"

And thanks to the spiritual heritage and legacy that his father has passed down to him, Preston can boldly move forward in the divine purpose to which he has been called. That includes a personal goal of reaching young people with the message of hope that can be found in the Gospel of Christ.

"Kids these days don't have that," Preston says. "They don't have the hope in knowing that God loves them. There's power in Jesus that we have access to through prayer and the Word. That's one of the reasons why I like to go out and speak. It's one of the reasons why I wanted to make it to where I am now, so I would have a platform to go talk to kids. It's such a passion of mine to see the faces of kids and think back to when I was that age and remember the hopes that I had.

"I'm still geeked on what I get to do now. I got to play on *Monday Night Football*. That's a dream come true. And for someone like me who really felt God move in my life from when I first started playing sports until now, it's really important for me to go out and talk to kids and tell them to dream just as big and help give them the confidence in knowing that God is faithful, and He will take you to where He wants you to be. It may not be exactly the plans you have, but He has great plans for all that He has called according to His purpose."

In his outreach efforts, Preston has learned first-hand the harsh reality that pervades the lives of so many young people today. He understands how so many of the ones he meets don't have the advantages of the kind of family heritage that he was blessed to enjoy. That's what makes the task at hand—helping kids learn about integrity and biblical values—so much more difficult.

"That's the hardest job," he says. "You just look at the moral standing of our world today and the stuff that you see on TV and all the things that young people are exposed to today. It was hard when I was in middle school and high school to stand firm on my principles. I can only imagine how much harder it is now. Christian values and Christian morals are getting increasingly further away from the norm in society."

Preston realizes that he is just one person trying to make a difference, but he also knows that there are thousands of people around the country working toward the same goal. Some of these people who were a key part of *his* life came via his involvement with Fellowship of Christian Athletes. Chris Brown, in particular, helped him through some difficult times while attending Illinois.

And as young athletes are searching for direction that maybe can't be found at home, Preston suggests going straight to the source.

"Cling to God," Preston advises. "Cling to the things that you know to be true in terms of the Word. You've also got to find something like FCA to get involved with and try to find people who are like-minded with you. I had a few people growing up who had goals like I had and were willing to sacrifice certain things and maybe sacrifice being part of the cool crowd. Try to find friends like that—people who will stand strong with you in times when you feel like you're standing out like a sore thumb because you don't really believe the same things that other people believe."

Ultimately, Preston didn't just take on the legacy that his father passed to him; he boldly and courageously took it from him—just like the anchor in a relay race might grab the baton from a teammate and then run toward the finish line with reckless abandon. Many times he came to a crossroads where he easily could have rejected the integrity that his father had instilled in him. It took challenging situations (like the defining moment he faced as a freshman football player) to help shake off his desire for the things of the world and replace that with a desire to follow in the footsteps of both his earthly father and his heavenly Father.

131

"For those who don't have the father figure that I had, it's really no different how God does it," Preston says. "He's going to get your attention one way or another. It could be through the booming voice that my dad had when he called me off the racquetball court, or it could be something small. It's always interesting to see how God gets His will accomplished. He's going to do it one way or another."

TRAINING TIME

1. What are some of the valuable lessons about integrity that Duke Preston learned from his father? Can you describe a time when someone taught you the meaning of integrity with their words or actions?

2. Read Colossians 3:22-24. How does what this Scripture relates differ from the mentality of so many people in the public eye? What are some ways that you can keep an eternal perspective in various aspects of your life?

3. When Preston visited his father's old neighborhood, it helped him understand the correlation between humility and integrity. How are those two characteristics intertwined? How can a lack of humility interfere with the pursuit of integrity?

4. Read 2 Timothy 1:2-7. Why do you think Paul felt compelled to recognize the example of integrity set by Timothy's mother and grandmother? How can those kinds of examples fortify the "spirit of power, of love and of self-discipline" described in verse 7?

5. How much responsibility should be placed on those teaching integrity? How much responsibility do you think should be placed on those being taught integrity? What are some ways that you can "catch" integrity from someone else?

"I was always kind of a fat kid growing up. I wasn't necessarily obese, but I was just a heavy kid. I remember when I was about eight years old; it was spring and getting close to the end of the school year. Our whole family went to the park one day, and my mom said, 'Duke, why don't you run a lap around the track?' So I got about halfway around, and I was just gassed. My hands were on my knees, and I was just spent. So that whole summer, my dad would take me to the track three or four days a week. We started with one lap and then moved up to two laps and three laps. And by the end of the summer, I was running eight-minute miles. He never made me go, but I hated it. I remember I would lie in bed every morning, and I was thinking, *Please, God. Please don't let him wake up. I just want to lay here in bed.* And for sure, he'd come in my room and say, 'C'mon, man.' So I'd get up and run. That taught me at a really young age how hard work pays off and brings results. Even at that age, I had lofty goals for what I wanted to do athletically. That was just a way to help me realize how hard work pays off and how staying dedicated to something can bear fruit."

—Duke Preston

STAYING THE COURSE

Aaron Baddeley
PGA Golfer

Brothers, I do not consider myself to have taken hold of it.
But one thing I do: forgetting what is behind and reaching forward
to what is ahead, I pursue as my goal the prize promised
by God's heavenly call in Christ Jesus.

PHILIPPIANS 3:13-14

Never give in, never give in, never, never, never, never—
in nothing, great or small, large or petty—never give in except
to convictions of honour and good sense.

WINSTON CHURCHILL

Depending on the golf course, the average PGA golfer will take roughly 280 shots during a four-round tournament. Within each one of those swings there is an enormous amount of pressure. For some players, one shot could make the difference between picking up a weekend paycheck and making an early exit—the difference between retaining a tour card and going back to qualifying school.

Aaron Baddeley fully understands all of the ramifications that accompany golf's micromanaged scoring system. He has missed the cut by one stroke and made the cut by the same paper-thin margin. Baddeley never takes his position on the PGA for granted but somehow finds relief from the inherent stress with a special technique.

"There are times that I get over a shot, and I'm a little worried about it," Baddeley says. "Then you're like, *I don't have a spirit of fear. I've got a spirit of power, love and a sound mind.* Sometimes I write Scriptures on my glove as a reminder. Sometimes you can get to a certain shot, and you're a little wary about it, and you can quote Scripture, and get a peace about it."

Baddeley's paraphrasing of 2 Timothy 1:7 is a far cry from the lackadaisical attitude toward prayer he maintained throughout most of his life as a teenager and young adult in his early twenties. Baddeley actually had parents who set a solid Christian example for him.

Born in Lebanon, New Hampshire, Baddeley's father, Ron, worked as chief mechanic for Mario Andretti's race team. The family moved back to its native Australia when the young Baddeley was nearing his third birthday. To this day, Baddeley enjoys dual citizenship, though he represents Australia in professional golf. Back in Melbourne, he spent the formative years of his childhood in a family that regularly attended a church where his father was an elder and his mom was a Sunday School teacher.

"I remember giving my life to Christ when I was 12 years old," Baddeley says. "I was at a youth outreach where a famous Australian rules football player was speaking. But after that, I just went through the motions."

While a relationship with God quickly became an afterthought, Baddeley's strong desire for athletic competition became king in his life. He started playing golf under the guidance of his grandmother Jean when he was eight years old, but he didn't get serious about the sport until he was 14. Up until that point, Baddeley says, he was a serious cricket player.

But once golf finally won him over, Baddeley grew more and more obsessed with it. Not only did he work tirelessly on the fundamentals of the game, but he also began studying the game's history and developing a thirst for knowledge of golf's biggest stars.

"I knew everyone, especially the big names," Baddeley says. "I watched so much golf, it was ridiculous. I could tell you every shot Nick Price hit in the last round when he won the PGA [Championship] at Southern Hills [in Tulsa, Oklahoma, in 1992]. I could tell you the commentary. Ever since I started playing golf, I just loved watching it."

By the time Baddeley was 18, he was one of Australia's top amateur golfers. That fact was solidified when he won the 1999 Australian Open—the youngest player ever to do so. But not long after his crowning achievement, Baddeley fell into a slump. He admits that 10 months later, he was tempted to "quit the game." Instead, he decided to recommit himself to golf and defended his title by winning the 2000 Australian Open—this time as a professional.

Five months later, he played in his first PGA Tour event at the Honda Classic. One might assume the college-aged youngster would have been just a little bit intimidated by the prospect of playing alongside golf's greatest players. But that was far from the truth. When he was younger, Baddeley had played with legendary Australian golfer Greg Norman. He also befriended Phil Mickelson; and the two practiced together in Scottsdale, Arizona, on a regular basis.

But it didn't take long for his new life in the United States to lose its luster. During the 2000 season, Baddeley struggled to keep the pace and made the cut just once in nine starts. Perhaps the best moment during that stretch on the PGA Tour was receiving a special invitation to play in the Masters (the youngest player to ever receive such an honor) and the thrilling opportunity to play a round with Tiger Woods. Otherwise, a tie for fifty-seventh place at the Honda Classic was the one consolation in an otherwise disappointing season.

"This was going to be the best year of my life," Baddeley remembers. "This is where I wanted to be. This is where I'd dreamed of being for six years. I came over and in 10 months I wanted to quit the game. It turned out to be the worst year of my life."

In 2001, Baddeley regained his winning stroke in time to capture the Greg Norman Holden International—a tournament hosted by and named after his boyhood hero and mentor. He also played in nine PGA Tour events that year, but barely fared better than the year before—by making two cuts. At that point, any reasonable golfer might have stressed out over form, training or even equipment. Instead, Baddeley says it was an unusual life decision that sparked positive change.

"In 2002, I felt like God was calling me to take a dating vow," Baddeley says. "I felt like He was asking me to give up dating for a season. So for the next six months, I didn't go out with any girls. I did it without even thinking. That was the point where God really got a hold of me. That's where I really started to press in and seek Him."

Baddeley stayed in touch with his pastor from Australia, who mentored him through the process by email. Throughout the six months, he learned invaluable nuggets of wisdom about dating and about himself. But most importantly, Baddeley began experiencing a personal relationship with God like never before.

"From then on, I have been growing closer to the Lord," he says. "It was during that time of committing to Him and learning more about what the Bible said and about God that I learned how personable God is and how much He enjoys someone who is committed to Him. To maintain the vow and not break it, I had to be obedient, and it was through the obedience that I learned so much."

Not only did Baddeley grow spiritually and emotionally during those six months, but he also found that his golf game began improving as well. On the 2002 Nationwide Tour, he finished runner-up in three tournaments and earned his way onto the PGA Tour by placing tenth on the circuit's money list. Baddeley admits that the

Nationwide Tour wasn't exactly where he wanted to be, but quickly realized that God had orchestrated the location and timing all along.

"That point was the best year of my life," Baddeley recalls. "Having a strong relationship with the Lord allowed me to have peace and happiness and enjoyment. The difference was obviously in my improved relationship with Christ. My friends noticed too, and I was able to share with them that the difference was Jesus."

As Baddeley's relationship with God grew, so did his success on the PGA Tour. As a rookie in 2003, he claimed three top-10 finishes, including the Sony Open in Hawaii, where he lost a two-hole playoff to Ernie Els. In 2004, Baddeley again narrowly missed his first tour victory with a second-place finish to Heath Slocum at the Chrysler Classic of Tucson, but he did maintain his PGA status by finishing in the top 125 on the money list.

In 2005, Baddeley continued his slow rise as one of the tour's next young contenders. But the dating vow he had taken three years earlier—and the lessons learned from it—finally paid off when he married the love of his life, Richelle, on Easter Sunday.

"I know that everything's in His time," Baddeley says. "You've got the promises of the Word that all things work for the good. When things don't go your way, you can be like, *All right, there's something going on here.* 'Lord, show me what You're trying to teach me.' The promises in the Word are what give you so much peace."

For Baddeley, 2006 was truly a breakout year. One year and one day after his wedding, he claimed his first PGA Tour title at the Verizon Heritage. The Sunday morning before the final round, Baddeley spoke at a sunrise service near the eighteenth green. After the win, his faith in Jesus became the centerpiece of every interview. The 2007 season was even more successful, with a second PGA Tour victory taking place at the FBR Open in Phoenix. Baddeley ended the year with more than $3 million in tournament earnings and finished sixth in the inaugural FedEx Cup standings.

Suffice it to say, Baddeley has been at both ends of the spectrum. He has missed the cut and lost his shot at the big time. On the flipside, he has won prestigious tournaments, earned big paychecks and has shared the course with golf's greatest players. The precarious balance between success and failure has helped the young Aussie fully understand the biblical truth found in Romans 8:38-39.

"Nothing can separate us from His love," Baddeley says. "You could shoot 85-85, and you can go to the prayer closet, and He's going to be there. He's still going to want to talk to you. He's still going to want to hold you. In this day and age, performance is something that people struggle with, and I struggle with it as well. I wouldn't say I'm immune to it at all. There are times that you put a value on your performance."

In those times when Baddeley is tempted to let the insecurities of human nature creep back into his heart, he reminds himself of his personal definition of integrity: "To live according to God's Word."

Baddeley's first real-life examples of biblical integrity were his parents. More recently, he has relied on the models found in his wife, Richelle, and in close friend John Bevere—a noted author, speaker and minister. Others that Baddeley has learned from include fellow PGA star Tom Lehman, longtime PGA chaplain Larry Moody, and Tommy Barnett, senior pastor at First Assembly of God in Phoenix. And one of the biggest lessons he's extrapolated from that impressive cast of characters is the importance of maintaining a high level of integrity in order to open the door to people's hearts.

"Live what you preach," Baddeley says. "As a Christian, you're always held under a microscope. You really have to be careful. You've got to live upright and holy. That's the biggest witnessing tool. It's just what James [2:26] is saying: 'Faith without works is dead.' You've got to live what your faith is."

Baddeley says that his biggest tool in reaching others is simply telling them the testimony of his life. "They can't argue with it because it's my testimony," he adds. But even more important to Baddeley is that he constantly does his best to go where God is leading him, and that means listening to that ever-present Guide.

"I definitely want to listen to what's going on inside, what the Holy Spirit is trying to say," Baddeley says. "Then I just tell them about Jesus. I often start out talking about church. I'll ask them where they go to church, and if they don't go, it opens the door."

Baddeley knows too well that effective outreach can be strengthened or weakened by the believer's integrity or lack thereof. That's why one of his favorite passages of Scripture is 1 Peter 1:15-16: "But, as the One who called you is holy, you also are to be in all your conduct; for it is written, Be holy, because I am holy."

"I love this because it's the Lord's call on all our lives," Baddeley says. "He is our example. He is our standard. He is who we need in our life to live a life of integrity and one that pleases God. I am supposed to strive to live my life like Jesus did."

One thing Baddeley has come to understand early in his life is the importance of commitment. It requires commitment to excellence in training and practice in order to become an elite golfer. It likewise requires commitment to make a modern marriage work. And commitment especially applies when it comes to one's character and the upholding of one's relationship with God.

"You need to be committed to walking in integrity and walking in God's commands," he says. "I feel what challenges me is that I need to be ready to be committed all the time, not some of the time, but 100 percent of the time. I need to be committed to integrity and God's commands, because that's what He expects from us. I feel like it's also important to make sure my heart is committed daily to walking along the right path."

According to Baddeley, the blessings that come from a life of integrity are innumerable and can be found in the here and now and in the ever after. But just as countless as those gifts can be, the dangers of turning from God's holiness are likewise immeasurable and something that all followers of Christ should avoid at all costs.

"By breaking commitments, we sin against God and against what He calls us to be," Baddeley says. "When we allow sin to enter our life by breaking commitments, we give the devil a foothold in our life. The more we sin, the easier it becomes, and the more of a habit it becomes. Then before we know it, we are walking in the wrong direction, and our integrity is no longer intact; and we are living a life that does not please God."

In the world of high-stakes professional sports, Baddeley has seen the highest highs and the lowest lows. He knows the difference between a life that relies on God and a life that trusts in oneself, and his level of commitment is no longer determined by external facts of life. That's why he says the best way to learn about integrity—and the most effective tools for a long-term spiritual commitment—is simply to read the pages of God's Word and to spend significant amounts of time in prayer.

"By doing this, God's Word becomes implanted in our heart," Baddeley says. "When that happens, we are able to live a life of integrity and a life that pleases God. When we commit ourselves to being obedient to God's Word, we can all walk in a life of integrity."

TRAINING TIME

1. Read 2 Timothy 1:7. Can you describe some situations that cause you to worry? What reassurance does this Scripture give you for times like that? What is the significance of Jesus' reference to the spirits of "power, love and sound judgment"?

2. Baddeley tells about a dating vow he took in 2002 that led to him not dating for six months. Has God ever taken you to extreme measures? If so, what kind of impact did they have on your relationship with Him?

3. Baddeley says, "By breaking commitments, we sin against God and against what He calls us to be." What is the connection between commitment and integrity? What are some ways that you can stay accountable to your commitments?

4. Read Psalm 27:4. What does this passage suggest was the key behind David's devotion to God? How can you take David's example of commitment—in spite of his imperfection—and apply it to your life?

5. Read Philippians 3:13-14. Why do you think it is dangerous to dwell too much on the past? How does this passage inspire you to focus on the future? What part does commitment and integrity play in this process of pursuing "the prize promised by God's heavenly call in Christ Jesus"?

"I really enjoy speaking. In 2004, I was in Vegas, and God really confronted me on the issue of gifts and callings. Through that, a message came about that I've been sharing. Everyone's been given a gift, whether that's being a speaker, whether that's being able to take care of someone, whether that's being able to read and write. Whatever the gift is, we've been given a calling to be a golfer or be a preacher or be a nurse. Take hold of that and use what God's given you, and don't change until God tells you otherwise. God's put you there for a specific purpose. I felt like I wanted to get more into the ministry because I enjoyed speaking and sharing Christ. But that's not where He wanted me. That's why I'm constantly trying to make sure I'm in the right spot. You've got to be where God wants you to be. He's given me a gift to play golf, and I need to use that to the maximum. God's not going to go hit practice balls for me. He's not going to go hit the putts for me. I've got to do that, but He's going to be there to help me. People really respond well to the message that I share about giftings and callings. But for right now, I've been called to golf. That's where the Lord's got me. Until He tells me otherwise, that's where I'm going to stay."

—Aaron Baddeley

CHARACTER COUNTS

John Wooden
Former UCLA Head Men's Basketball Coach

Blessed are the pure in heart, because they will see God.
MATTHEW 5:8

When wealth is lost, nothing is lost; when health is lost, something is lost; when character is lost, all is lost.
BILLY GRAHAM

One of Coach John Wooden's favorite Bible figures is Job. That might seem an odd choice for the man known for leading the UCLA Bruins to a record-smashing 10 NCAA men's basketball championships, producing a slew of All-Americans and developing NBA stars such as Lew Alcindor (now Kareem Abdul Jabbar), Bill Walton, Walt Hazzard, Marques Johnson and Henry Bibby.

But for the people who know Wooden best, the choice isn't the least bit surprising, as can be extracted from one of the Bible's most straightforward passages: "There was a man in the country of Uz named Job. He was a man of perfect integrity, who feared God and turned away from evil" (Job 1:1).

That verse might seem simple on the surface, but the unique events of Job's life truly make his pursuit of integrity compelling. Because of Job's character, God had placed a hedge of protection around him and his family. He was blessed with health, wealth and prosperity. But Satan questioned that faithfulness, so he asked for an opportunity to test Job and find out if he truly loved God.

Satan attacked Job with great sickness and immense poverty. He even took the lives of his children. While Job cried out to God and questioned his fate, this man of integrity never turned his back on the Lord, and ultimately he found a way to worship God despite the traumatic circumstances. Eventually, Satan was vanquished from Job's life. Job's health was restored, and his material possessions were increased.

147

Like Job, who struggled in his faith during those hardships, Wooden candidly admits that there have been times in his life when he failed to live up to the highest standards of integrity. While those moments have been few and far between, he has always learned from his mistakes and been able to use them to not only better his own life but also the lives of those around him.

"At UCLA, I was tempted to be dishonest many times," Wooden says. "Mostly I resisted, but there was one situation of which I am not very proud. An opposing coach repeatedly sent the wrong shooter to the free-throw line. Since the opposing coach got away with this illegal maneuver, I tried it too. But I was not so good at being stealthy—

and I got caught. I regret giving in to temptation, not only because I got caught but primarily because I did not stay true to my standards."

Wooden also had a smoking habit that began during his World War II military service and plagued him early in his coaching career. He would quit during basketball season, and he never smoked in front of his players. But he felt convicted and realized that he needed to do a better job teaching the impressionable athletes not just about basketball but also about living a life of integrity.

"A leader's most powerful ally is his or her own example," Wooden says. "There is hypocrisy to the phrase, 'Do as I say, not as I do.' I refused to make demands on my boys that I wasn't willing to live out in my own life. Leadership from a base of hypocrisy undermines respect, and if people don't respect you, they won't willingly follow you."

Wooden's standards come straight from the Bible, which he began reading as a teenager. By the time he was in college, he was reading it on a daily basis. This habit continued on throughout his marriage to his wife, Nellie, of 53 years (she passed away in 1985).

Wooden dove into the Bible because he enjoyed spending time in God's Word. To him, it was never the arduous task that sadly skews most Christians' perception about reading the Bible. Instead, Wooden's joyful participation in Bible study helped him to understand the purpose of God's commandments and empowered him to live out the truth found in Psalm 119:11: "I have treasured Your word in my heart so that I may not sin against You."

"The Lord created each of us to be unique, and because of that, many of us have differing values," Wooden says. "But I believe God put some absolutes in place. The Ten Commandments reflect some of His absolutes. When we violate those absolutes, we fail as people of integrity."

According to Wooden, one of the most important pillars of integrity is honesty, which he describes as "doing the things that we know are right and not giving into the temptation to do the things that we know are wrong."

Of course, Wooden fully realizes that honesty isn't a natural occurrence in the human DNA. Once Adam and Eve sinned in the Garden of Eden by disobeying God and then lying about it, mankind was instantly plagued with the hereditary disease of dishonesty. Jesus pointed out this harsh reality to the religious leaders of the day when He rebuked their self-righteous attitudes in Matthew 12:34, saying, "How can you speak good things when you are evil? For the mouth speaks from the overflow of the heart."

It's the condition of the heart that produces truth or lies, good or bad choices, or healthy or destructive behaviors. But the root cause can always be traced back to what a person has allowed into his or her heart through the portals of the ears and the eyes, which are then filtered through the mind. "Integrity in its simplest form is purity of intention," Wooden says. "It's keeping a clean conscience. Purity of intention is really a reflection of the heart. The heart of a person with integrity always wants to do what's right, once he or she is sure what 'right' is."

In his 40 years of coaching high school and college basketball, Wooden saw every kind of personality and character type imaginable. He coached players who had something he calls "selective integrity," but he also worked with athletes who had a firm grasp on the concept. At the end of the day, it was the ones who chose the narrow road who received the greatest rewards.

"When we have integrity, we are not going to do anything that will be demeaning to anybody else, either on or off the court," Wooden says. "And with integrity, we will never consider letting our teammates down. I think I can safely say that the more the quality of integrity was represented in the best seven or eight players on each of my teams, the better their team play became."

While Wooden enjoyed great success based on the team play produced by young men with outstanding integrity, winning championships and personal accolades has never measured up to the spiritual blessings that accompany the life of Christ-centered character. In fact, it was Jesus Himself who in the famed Sermon on the Mount said, "Blessed are the pure in heart, because they will see God" (Matthew 5:8).

But beyond the eternal ramifications of honesty and integrity, Wooden believes that there are immense benefits here on Earth for those who choose to embrace truth at all times. "Honesty is not only the best policy, but it is also the best therapy," Wooden says. "Telling the truth and being true to ourselves not only enhance our relations with others and with God, but they also make us feel good about ourselves."

TRAINING TIME

1. Read Job 1:1. When you're dealing with tough times, what effect do those circumstances tend to have on your character? What gives you strength and peace of mind during such trials?

2. Read Psalm 119:11. What truth found in this passage is the key to living with integrity? What are some specific ways that your study of the Bible has helped you make good decisions in life?

3. Wooden says, "Integrity in its simplest form is purity of intention." Do you agree with that statement? Read Matthew 12:34. What commentary do you think Jesus was trying to make about the condition of the heart with regard to one's actions? Do you think it is possible to serve others but with wrong motivations?

4. What are some tough decisions that could challenge one's integrity? How does one's willingness (or lack of willingness) to face the consequences of such a decision speak to the issue of motive and intent (or purity of heart)?

5. Read Matthew 5:8. What does this Scripture state is the ultimate benefit of having a pure heart? How might that blessing come to fruition in this life? What about in the next life?

"When I returned to Indiana after the war, I turned down jobs at two very fine high schools and accepted a position at Indiana State University instead. I hoped that if I did well, I would have the opportunity to get a coaching job at a Big Ten school or perhaps another major university. My Indiana State teams did very well, and after the second year, the University of Minnesota and UCLA had openings. Both schools offered me jobs. I was going to take the Minnesota job, but there was something that had to be worked out. UCLA was getting impatient. They wanted an answer by the middle of the afternoon. I told Minnesota that they would have to let me know an hour before UCLA needed an answer. I never received the call. I didn't know it, but a snowstorm had knocked out the lines. UCLA did call, and I accepted their offer. The Minnesota people got through to me an hour later and said that all the details had been resolved. I thanked them for the offer but told them I could not take it. I was sorry, but I wouldn't break my word to UCLA. I came to UCLA not as a first choice. I came because a college teammate, who now was on the UCLA football coaching staff, thought there would be a future there. I came because there was a snowstorm and Minnesota's people could not get through to me. And I came because I had given my word."

—John Wooden

THANKS

Fellowship of Christian Athletes would like to give honor and glory to our Lord and Savior Jesus Christ for the opportunities we have been given to impact so many lives and for everyone who has come alongside us in this ministry.

The four core values are at the heart of what we do and teach. Many people have helped make this series of books on these values a reality. We extend a huge thanks to Chad Bonham for his many hours of hard work in interviewing, writing, compiling and editing. These books would not have been possible without him. Thanks also to Chad's wife, Amy, and his two young sons, Lance and Cole (who was born just about the time the manuscript went to the publisher).

We also want to thank the following people and groups for their vital contributions: Les Steckel, Tony Dungy, Jackie Cook, the Indianapolis Colts, Shaun Alexander, Lane Gammel, the Seattle Seahawks, Todd Gowin, Mark Heligman, John Wooden, Lorenzo Romar, Jamee Ashburn, the University of Washington basketball program, Duke Preston, Teddi Domann, Kayla Ravenkamp, Domann & Pittman Football, Jon Kitna, Tom Valente, the Detroit Lions, Josh Davis, Laura Wilkinson, Heather Novickis, Octagon, Jennifer Lowery, USA Diving, Aaron Baddeley, Bobby Jones, Wendy Ward, Drew Dyck, *New Man Magazine* and Dave Bartlett.

Thanks to the entire FCA staff, who every day faithfully serve coaches and athletes. Thanks to our CEO and president, Les Steckel, for believing in this project. Thanks to the Home Office staff: Bethany Hermes, Tom Rogeberg, Jill Ewert, Shea Vailes and Ken Williams. Thanks also to Bill Greig III, Bill Schultz, Steven Lawson, Mark Weising, Aly Hawkins and everyone at Regal Books.

IMPACTING THE WORLD FOR CHRIST THROUGH SPORTS

Since 1954, the Fellowship of Christian Athletes has challenged athletes and coaches to impact the world for Jesus Christ. FCA is cultivating Christian principles in local communities nationwide by encouraging, equipping, and empowering others to serve as examples and make a difference. Reaching more than 2 million people annually on the professional, college, high school, junior high and youth levels, FCA has grown into the largest sports ministry in the world. Through FCA's Four Cs of Ministry—coaches, campus, camps, and community—and the shared passion for athletics and faith, lives are changed for current and future generations.

Fellowship of Christian Athletes

8701 Leeds Road • Kansas City, MO 64129

www. fca.org • fca@fca.org • 1-800-289-0909

COMPETITORS FOR CHRIST

Fellowship of Christian Athletes Competitor's Creed

I am a Christian first and last.
I am created in the likeness of God Almighty to bring Him glory.
I am a member of Team Jesus Christ.
I wear the colors of the cross.

I am a Competitor now and forever.
I am made to strive, to strain, to stretch and to succeed in the arena of competition.
I am a Christian Competitor and as such, I face my challenger with the face of Christ.

I do not trust in myself.
I do not boast in my abilities or believe in my own strength.
I rely solely on the power of God.
I compete for the pleasure of my Heavenly Father, the honor
of Christ and the reputation of the Holy Spirit.

My attitude on and off the field is above reproach—my conduct beyond criticism.
Whether I am preparing, practicing or playing,
I submit to God's authority and those He has put over me.
I respect my coaches, officials, teammates, and competitors out of respect for the Lord.

My body is the temple of Jesus Christ.
I protect it from within and without.
Nothing enters my body that does not honor the Living God.
My sweat is an offering to my Master. My soreness is a sacrifice to my Savior.

I give my all—all the time.
I do not give up. I do not give in. I do not give out.
I am the Lord's warrior—a competitor by conviction and a disciple of determination.
I am confident beyond reason because my confidence lies in Christ.
The results of my effort must result in His glory.

Let the competition begin.
Let the glory be God's.

Sign the Creed • Go to www.fca.org

Fellowship of Christian Athletes Coach's Mandate

Pray as though nothing of eternal value is going
to happen in my athletes' lives unless God does it.

Prepare each practice and game as giving "my utmost for His highest."

Seek not to be served by my athletes for personal gain, but seek
to serve them as Christ served the church.

Be satisfied not with producing a good record, but with producing good athletes.

Attend carefully to my private and public walk with God, knowing that the
athlete will never rise to a standard higher than that being lived by the coach.

Exalt Christ in my coaching, trusting the Lord will then draw athletes to Himself.

Desire to have a growing hunger for God's Word, for personal
obedience, for fruit of the spirit and for saltiness in competition.

Depend solely upon God for transformation—one athlete at a time.

Preach Christ's word in a Christ-like demeanor, on and off the field of competition.

Recognize that it is impossible to bring glory to both myself
and Christ at the same time.

Allow my coaching to exude the fruit of the Spirit,
thus producing Christ-like athletes.

Trust God to produce in my athletes His chosen purposes,
regardless of whether the wins are readily visible.

Coach with humble gratitude, as one privileged to be God's coach.